THE
COMPLETE NONSENSE
OF
EDWARD LEAR

edited

and introduced by

HOLBROOK JACKSON

ff

faber and faber

First published in 1947
by Faber and Faber Limited
3 Queen Square London WCIN 3AU

First published in this edition in 2001

ISBN 0–571–20736–7

Printed and bound in Great Britain by
Mackays of Chatham plc, Chatham, Kent

2 4 6 8 10 9 7 5 3

SELF-PORTRAIT OF
THE LAUREATE OF NONSENSE

How pleasant to know Mr. Lear!
    Who has written such volumes of stuff!
Some think him ill-tempered and queer,
    But a few think him pleasant enough.

His mind is concrete and fastidious,
    His nose is remarkably big;
His visage is more or less hideous,
    His beard it resembles a wig.

He has ears, and two eyes, and ten fingers,
    Leastways if you reckon two thumbs;
Long ago he was one of the singers,
    But now he is one of the dumbs.

He sits in a beautiful parlour,
    With hundreds of books on the wall;
He drinks a great deal of Marsala,
    But never gets tipsy at all.

He has many friends, laymen and clerical;
    Old Foss is the name of his cat;
His body is perfectly spherical,
    He weareth a runcible hat.

When he walks in a waterproof white,
    The children run after him so!
Calling out, 'He's come out in his night-
    Gown, that crazy old Englishman, oh!'

He weeps by the side of the ocean,
    He weeps on the top of the hill;
He purchases pancakes and lotion,
    And chocolate shrimps from the mill.

He reads but he cannot speak Spanish,
    He cannot abide ginger-beer:
Ere the days of his pilgrimage vanish,
    How pleasant to know Mr. Lear!

EDWARD LEAR

CONTENTS

INTRODUCTION

EDWARD LEAR:
LAUREATE OF NONSENSE

By HOLBROOK JACKSON

1

Just over a hundred years ago the children of England (and also many older folk) were surprised into entertainment by the appearance 'out of the blue' of an oblong book of hilarious rhymes and still more hilarious pictures by an author hitherto unknown to the general public. This fantastic collection of rhymes-without-reason was an instantaneous success, and Edward Lear's *Book of Nonsense* had given a local habitation and a name to one of the oldest and most persistent of human faculties. Its author, like an earlier poet, awoke to find himself famous—but in an entirely different branch of art from that by which he sought to earn a living, and he remains its un-challenged laureate. The literature of nonsense has grown in quality as well as quantity during the past century but the whole-hearted abandonment of sense, as formalised by Edward Lear, is still the classical example of this curious and amusing art.

There are several ways of approaching the fine arts and particu-larly that of an artist so peculiar as Edward Lear, for although the entertainment value of the *Book of Nonsense* and its pendants is obvious, the personality and motives behind that work will repay examination. Such an examination is tempting because Lear was no ordinary writer turning out humorous books for a living, nor were those books his only productions; on the contrary his nonsense began as the sideline of a professional life devoted to the illustration of books, mainly ornithological, and the pursuit of the picturesque for those landscapes which were latterly his main source of revenue. At the same time nonsense was not merely an occasional, still less an idle occupation. What appeared to begin and end in the casual amusement of children was actually a method of amusing, or, better, diverting himself. His excursions into the realm of nonsense were certainly occasional but the occasions were so frequent as to pervade the whole of his life, ultimately becoming a continuous as well as a formal medium of expression. Nonsense was the safety-valve of his consciousness responding to most of his approaches to himself and his environment. It became ultimately a world in itself specially created by him as a refuge from the trials and irritations of life: ill-health, lack of means, and, above all, an over-strung sensibility. Nonsense was thus Lear's Ivory Tower and it was far more accessible than most retreats of the kind and its peace could be enjoyed without fuss or ceremony in most emergencies. It was as though he lived a double life, one in the realm of sense and the other in that of nonsense; and he had the power of transmuting himself from one to the other at will, a gift which he exercised almost continuously as his familiar letters prove. Most of those who know the *Book of Nonsense* and even one or more of the sequels think of Lear solely as writer and illustrator of amusing limericks; but that was only one form of his nonsense. In addition and equally important are his nonsense alphabets and vocabularies, poems and pictures, which comprise nonsense geography, natural history, botany, and anthropology. He depended largely upon his own subconscious promptings for the flora and fauna of this funny cosmogony, but was not averse from annexing birds and animals from nature which happened to approximate to his own nonsensical conceptions. Thus pelicans and parrots, seals and rhinoceroses and other queer creatures associated appropriately with his Dongs and Pobbles and Quangle-Wangles :

> *Herons and Gulls and Cormorants black*
> *Cranes and Flamingoes with scarlet back,*

> *Plovers and Storks, and Geese in clouds,*
> *Swans and Dilberry Ducks in crowds.*

He even nonsensified himself and his cat in verse, and in those humorous drawings which are a characteristic and happy feature of a large number of his letters to intimate friends.

2

There was something preposterous about Edward Lear, amiably preposterous. He might have stepped out of one of his own nonsense books, and he seemed to know it and to make the most of it. He pokes fun at himself even when he is serious, and his letters dance with caricatures of his own plump figure, high-domed brow, and bushy whiskers. By profession he was a painter of birds and landscapes, by habit a wanderer, a humorist and a grumbler. He was, in fact, an artist, and if he had not been forced to fritter away his life in earning a living, he might have been a greater artist in his chosen profession of topographical illustrator. Instead of that he became famous for his side-lines—the sketches in water-colour incidental to his finished paintings, as well as to the nonsense rhymes and pictures which were his quaint lines of communication with his friends and their children, but which were themselves developed from an involuntary need for whimsical expression. Some inner conflict, aggravated by indifferent health and insufficient wealth drove him to cut capers with words and images and ideas. And so, by accident he becomes the laureate of nonsense, objectivising for his own relief and, as it happens, for our delight, that wilfulness which ever kept him a child in a world that was already in its second childhood.

He was born at Highgate on the 12th May 1812, and died in 1888 at San Remo, on the Italian Riviera where he had lived for eighteen years with his Albanian servant, Georgio Kokali, who had served him for nearly thirty years, and his famous cat, Foss, who had pre-deceased him by a few months at the advanced age of seventeen years.

Lear was the youngest of a family of twenty-one children, most of whom he outlived. Of the twenty-one, thirteen were girls and Edward was brought up by Ann, the eldest, who continued to mother him until her death when he was nearly fifty. His father was a stock-broker of Danish descent who speculated his way from affluence on Highgate Hill to poverty and the King's Bench Prison. His mother came from Durham, and was presumably English. Edward also attributed a liking for Irish character to the influence of a 'Gt.Gt.Gt.Gt.-Gt.Gt. grandfather' of Irish blood. So, remembering Hans Andersen, who was a Dane, and the supposed humour of Ireland, one may argue that Danish and Irish blood is a good mixture for the production of that kind of humorous fantasy which he called nonsense. But whatever his descent, Edward Lear possessed many of the characteristics of the more eccentric of wandering Englishmen, and neither he nor his peculiar brand of humour could have been produced anywhere but in England, the birthplace of the *Ingoldsby Legends*, the *Bab Ballads*, and *Alice in Wonderland*.

He never married; there is no evidence that he was attracted to women except as friends, and his works, literary and graphic, are as sexless as the artistic efforts of a child. He occasionally puzzles over the problem of marriage as he puzzles over so many things which are not quite obvious, but when he is in his forty-first year he rebukes any impulse to that end by reflecting that if he married he would 'paint less and less well', and further, this most determined and illustrious entertainer of children puts it on record that the thought of 'annual infants' of his own drives him 'wild'. In the same letter he argues as many bachelors, scared at the idea of a lonely old age, have done before him: 'If I attain to 65, and have an "establishment" with lots of spoons, etc., to offer—I *may* chain myself:—but surely not before. And alas! and seriously—when I look around my acquaintances—and few men have more, or know more intimately, do I see a majority of happy pairs? No, I don't. Single—I may have few pleasures—but married—many risks and miseries are semi-certainly in waiting—nor till the plot is played out can it be said that evils are not at hand.' Fear of matrimony is evidently a recurring whimsy, whose continued presence is revealed ten years later when he is living in Corfu, where he is attracted by a native girl and wishes, playfully, he were 'married to a clever good nice fat little Greek girl—and had 25 olive trees, some goats and a house'. 'But', he adds, 'the above girl, happily for herself, likes somebody else,' and there the matter ended and Edward Lear makes the pilgrimage of life alone, though not without friends, and the friendship of faithful servants, and the seventeen year long companionship of 'Old Foss', the cat, amusingly immortalised in so many of his drawings.

Although his education, according to modern standards, was inadequate, and he was earning a living as a commercial artist at fifteen, he managed to accumulate considerable culture. He could read or talk in at least half-a-dozen languages, including Greek both ancient and modern; and in addition to his skill as a painter of landscapes and his technical exactitude as an illustrator of birds, he composed and sang songs, wrote light verses, kept long diaries, wrote innumerable letters, and gave a new idiom to humorous drawing. He must also have had a gift for communicating his skill for at one time he was the art-master of Queen Victoria.

3

Those nonsense drawings and their attendant verse and prose reveal an invincible boyishness. On one side Lear was as old as the rocks he painted, on another as young as the children he loved or the child he awoke in the adults who loved him. This plump, bewhiskered man with high-domed brow, small, spectacled eyes and loose-fitting clothes was ineradicably childlike, although he must have looked what he would have called an 'old cove' nearly all his life. But in spite of that there was something of him that would not grow up: his peterpantheism was no pose. There was an unusual physical expression of this fortunate anomaly of prolonged adolescence. At the age of forty-one, the year, it will be recalled, in which the idea of marriage began to puzzle him, he 'cut two new teeth', and, after the attendant discomforts of this event, at first thought to be mumps, there was a renewal of health and spirits which he attributed to the belated infantile phenomenon.

Attempts at portraiture are fortunately unnecessary, for Lear loved self-dramatisation and has left several personal glimpses, both literary and graphic, the best of all that full-length self-portrait in verse which introduces this collection of his nonsense.

4

His varied gifts and dual character were encouraged by the manner of his upbringing, and although we have no cause for complaint, Edward Lear was always conscious of some masculine inadequacy. 'Brought up by women—and badly besides—and ill always,' he had no chance of 'manly improvements or exercise'. Yet, he says, 'I am always thanking God that I was never educated, for it seems to me that 999 of those who are so, expensively and laboriously, have lost all before they arrive at my age (47)—and remain like Swift's Strulbruggs—cut and dry for life,' whereas he seemed always to be on 'the threshold of knowledge'. Much as he loved quietness, inwardly and outwardly, he could not be still. He never lost the restlessness of childhood, and as he could not achieve the inward calm he craved, he denied its existence: 'As for content that is a loathesome slimy humbug —fit only for potatoes, very fat hogs—and fools generally. Let us pray fervently that we may never become such asses as to be contented.'

One of the most surprising things about him is that he managed to combine roving habits and impecuniosity with a considerable social status. It surprises even Lear himself. He cannot understand how 'such an asinine beetle' could have made so many friends. 'The immense variety of class and caste which I daily came in contact with in those days, would be a curious fact even in the life of a fool.' Many of his friends were patricians or 'swells', as he called them, and if he had wished he could have spent much more time than he did in the houses of the great and affluent, but being social rather than gregarious, he hated the 'bustle and lights and fuss of society' and soon tired of being a *flâneur*. Yet, pursued as he was by the demon of boredom, he must have friends as well as work, and contriving to enjoy both he went his grumbling, but, on the whole, cheerful way always rather surprised that 'such a queer beast' should have so many friends, and whimsically resentful at the drudgery which temperament and circumstances imposed upon him.

5

No more diligent artist ever lived. He had the concentration of a beaver and never liked parting with a job once he had started to gnaw it. During fifty years of his busy life, for instance, he made 200 illustrations for Tennyson's poems, but did not live to see any of them published.[1] Sometimes he suspected this laboriousness although he looked upon a 'totally unbroken application to poetical-topographical painting and drawing' as the 'universal panacea for the ills of life'.

The number of drawings he turned out on a sketching tour was astounding. In one year alone (1865) his 'outdoor work' comprised, '200 sketches in Crete, 145 in "the Corniche", and 125 at Nice, Antibes and Cannes.' He goes to India and in six months despatches to England 'no less than 560 drawings, large and small besides 9 small sketch books and 4 journals'. He was then sixty-two and described himself, with some justice, as 'a very energetic and frisky old cove'. When not travelling in search of the picturesque or working up his sketches, he is holding exhibitions of drawings and paintings from the sale of which he lived, or writing to his friends and patrons about work in progress and the attendant economic problems which were never entirely absent, and any spare time was devoted to the diaries which he kept for years, and those travel books[2] which he illustrated with some of his best drawings.

[1] A selection of these illustrations was published in 1889, the year after his death, with a Memoir by his old friend Franklin Lushington.
[2] *Views in Rome.* (1841); *Excursions in Italy* (1846); *Excursions in Italy, Second Series* (1846); *Journal of a Landscape Painter in Albania and Illyria* (1841); *Journal of a Landscape Painter in Southern Calabria* (1852); *Views in the Seven Ionian Islands* (1863); *Journal of a Landscape Painter in Corsica* (1870).

He lived to draw and paint and drew and painted to live, pretending to hate the necessity of having to go on day after day 'grinding' his 'nose off'. But although he talked little of art as such, and affected to belittle his own inspiration, his artistry was more than technique and it is a criticism of criticism that his drawings, particularly those in black and white and water-colours, should have been sidetracked rather than assessed. His habit of under-statement, as in the case of Anthony Trollope, is responsible for some of the posthumous neglect of his graphic work. His trick of looking upon himself as a recorder and 'topographer' rather than a creator, has been taken too literally. Self-depreciation was not a pose. Lear was as puzzled about his gifts as he was about marriage, or, indeed, about life. Conscious of 'being influenced to an extreme by everything in natural and physical life, i.e. atmosphere, light, shadow, and all the varieties of day and night', he wondered whether it was 'a blessing or the contrary', but decided, wisely enough, that 'things must be as they may, and the best is to make the best of what happens'. Like Pangloss he concludes that all is for the best in the best of all possible worlds and he certainly makes the best of this sensitiveness before the picturesque, grumbling much but demanding little beyond 'quiet and repose' so that he could get on with his work.

His idea of heaven is a place of charming landscapes without noise or fuss. 'When I go to heaven, if indeed I go—and am surrounded by thousands of polite angels—I shall say courteously "please leave me alone:—you are doubtless all delightful, but I do not wish to become acquainted with you;—let me have a park and a beautiful view of sea and hill, mountain and river, valley and plain, with no end of tropical foliage:—a few well-behaved cherubs to cook and keep the place clean—and—after I am quite established—say for a million or two years—an angel of a wife. Above all let there be no hens! No, not one! I give up eggs and roast chickens for ever".'

Uncertainty of income (for even the patronage of rich friends does not stabilise his finances) predisposes him to wish for a sinecure, and when, in 1863, Greece took to herself a king, Lear requests his friend Fortescue (afterwards Lord Carlingford) to 'write to Lord Palmerston to ask him to ask the Queen to ask the King of Greece to give' him a 'place' specially created, the title to be 'Lord High Bosh and Nonsense Producer . . . with permission to wear a fool's cap (or mitre)—three pounds of butter yearly and a little pig,—and a small donkey to ride on'. Before that, rumour having raised Mr. Gladstone to the Hellenic throne, Lear had threatened to 'write to Mr. G. for the appointment of Painter Laureate, and Grand Peripatetic Ass and Boshproducing Luminary' to the Greek Court.

The problem of finance was a constant irritant, and his wish to stabilise his income, though couched in the Learian nonsense idiom, was none the less a reality. But although he was chronically short of cash, he was never actually destitute or even poor. It was the lack of regular income rather than poverty which gave him a permanent feeling of insecurity. He was thus forced by circumstances to think unduly about money. Such a condition might have made him thrifty, which is often the first step to miserliness; but he was as generous as he was poor and continually helped the still poorer members of his family and others less closely related. 'I only wish for money to give it away,' is no idle boast, as we know from the records of many generous acts. His books contribute little to his variable income and it is to his landscapes that he turns for subsistence. He becomes a travelling showman of his own works, for at Corfu or Valetta or San Remo, he holds exhibitions, and in his later years there was a small permanent show of his pictures at Foord's Gallery in Wardour Street. But customers are shy and they do not always pay promptly. The position would have been still worse but for the support of regular patrons. His old friends are ever ready to help and to enlist the help of their friends, but even then there are lean periods, for, alas, 'private patronage must end in the natural course of things, but eating and drinking and clothing go on disagreeably continually.' Like William Blake he began his career as an illustrator of the works of others, and it was as a delineator of birds for the ornithologist John Gould that he attracted the attention of Edward Stanley, thirteenth Earl of Derby, the Whig statesman and scholar, known to literature as Bulwer Lytton's 'Rupert of debate'. Lord Derby engaged him to illustrate a book on the menagerie which was then a show-piece of the Stanley demesne at Knowsley near Liverpool. This commission was momentous, for it earned him the lifelong patronage of the noble family which has done many more serviceable things than lend its name to the most famous horse race in the world, not least the befriending of the quaint 'cove' whose work has already outlived the fame of his first kindly and illustrious patron. Edward Lear worked for no less than four successive Earls of Derby—but, more important still, he worked or rather played for the children in the household of his first patron, and by so doing achieved immortality. The first *Book of Nonsense* was composed to amuse the grandchildren, nephews and nieces of the thirteenth earl, to whose 'great-grandchildren, grand-nephews and grand-nieces', it is dedicated.

7

If ever a gifted man worked for a living it was Edward Lear, and, although he joked about his journeys, they were not jaunts but professional expeditions in search of the picturesque, with the object of turning it into marketable landscapes. He is in fact a pictorial merchant: a later Dr. Syntax—in search of a living. Scenery is the raw material of his trade. When trekking across Albania he is glad to leave the district of Peupli for Akhrida, where he hopes the scenery will be 'more valuable'. He is, as he declares in his *Corsican Journal*, a 'wandering painter—whose life's occupation is travelling for pictorial and topographic purposes'. But although he always makes a virtue of necessity, work is life to him. He fears idleness because it exposes him to boredom, and if he is capable of enduring the prophylactic of drudgery, he has no liking for the sedentary side of painting: 'No life is more *shocking* to me than sitting motionless like a petrified gorilla as to my body and limbs hour after hour—my hand meanwhile, peck peck pecking at billions of little dots and lines, while my mind is fretting and fuming through every moment of the weary day's work.'

He craves for movement as though his curiously active mind needed the companionship of an active body, for 'after all one isn't a potato', so perhaps it is better 'to run about continually like an ant'. It was nothing for him even when past his prime to walk fifteen and twenty miles a day, and to do an amount of sketching as well. The trade of landscape-painter was perhaps, after all, only the excuse for those laborious journeys in Albania, Greece, Corsica, Malta, Crete, Egypt, Corfu, Switzerland, Calabria and other parts of Italy, the French Riviera, and India. There are indications that he relished travel for its own sake and was always planning jaunts to ever more distant lands. It is probable, also, that he found in travel a means of relief from that mental stress which, as we shall see, was an underlying cause of his jocularity. The craving for movement is like a chronic desire to run away from himself. 'The more I read travels the more I want to move,' and he playfully invited his friend Fortescue to go with him to 'New Zealand, Tasmania and Lake Tchad'. As he grew older he believed that a sedentary life, after moving about as he had done for more than half a century, would 'infallibly finish' him 'off suddenly'. And although, he reflected, he might 'with equal suddenness be finished off if he moved about', he believed that 'a thorough change' would affect him 'far better rather than far worse. Whereby', he concludes, 'I shall go either to Sardinia, or India, or Jumsibobjiggle-quack this next winter as ever is.'

8

This restlessness was no doubt due to a nervous defect, for although Lear lived for well over seventy years, he always, and with reason, looked upon himself as an invalid and could not understand why he continued to survive after he was fifty. There was reason for these fears, whimsically as he often stated them, for he was an epileptic, and suffered also from chronic asthma and bronchitis, from which he ultimately died. But in spite of these defects, he had varying spells of comfortable health, and his ailments did not interfere with his love of wandering in strange lands, and of working continuously, and, on the whole, happily, at high pressure. At one time he is advised 'to take things easy' as he has 'the same complaint of the heart that my father died of', but there is no evidence that he took the advice. Asthma and bronchitis would have driven him to warmer and drier climates even if he had not been otherwise predisposed to travel. Some of his irascibility may be attributed to physical and nervous defects, but much of it is a normal if exaggerated love of grumbling, to which he invariably gave the characteristic Lear touch of nonsense. He is, however (after the manner of men who explode over trifles), inclined, like Walter Savage Landor, to congratulate himself on his composure. An instance occurs after a sunstroke in Italy: 'I often thank God', he said, 'that although he has given me a nature easily worried by small matters, yet in such cases as this I go on day after day quite calmly, only thankful that I do not suffer more.'

9

He has also numerous aversions, such as noises, crowds, hustle, gaiety, fools and bores, which are doubtless valetudinarian. Once he confesses that 'barring a few exceptionals', all human beings seem to be 'awful idiots'. Yet he is neither prig nor curmudgeon, and inclined to gently scan his brother man, but he enjoys company rather than 'society'. He is a worker but not a team-worker. 'Always accustomed from a boy to go my own way uncontrolled, I cannot help fearing that I should run rusty and sulky by reason of retinues and routines.' He repudiates the term Bohemian, but has 'just so much of that nature as it is perhaps impossible the artistic and poetic beast can be born without'.

Noise is the annoyance which comes in for the full blast of his whimsical invective, and it is the misplaced sounds of children, cats, poultry and music which annoy him most. He humours this sensitiveness all over Europe. In Paris: 'all the Devils in or out of Hell! four hundred and seventy-three cats at least are all at once making an infernal row in the garden close to my window. Therefore, being mentally decomposed, I shall write no more.' At a Swiss hotel the greatest drawback is the noise of children: 'the row of forty little ill-conducted beasts is simply frightful.' At Rome: all manner of things irritate him; among them the conversion of so many to the Roman Catholic faith and Manning preaching 'most atrocious sermons . . . to which nevertheless, all heaps of fools go'. But of all objectionable noises unwanted music inspires the fullness of his powers of vituperation. In Rome 'a vile beastly rottenheaded foolbegotten pernicious priggish screaming, tearing, roaring, perplexing, splitmecrackle, crachimecriggle insane ass of a woman is practising howling belowstairs with a brute of a singing master so horribly, that my head is nearly off'. And some few years later at Corfu he is 'much distressed by next door people who had twins babies and played the violin: but one of the twins died, and the other has eaten the fiddle—so all is peace'. As usual he compensates himself for these worries with a dose of nonsense, as, for example, the thought of ultimate calm among choice friends 'under a lotus tree a eating of ice creams and pelican pie, with our feet in a hazure coloured stream with the birds and beasts of Paradise a sporting around us'.

10

These irascibilities which play so large and so amusing a part in his letters, are mere whimsies when compared with his pecuniary anxieties. Money, always in 'short supply', is a stock subject of his letters, and at times, and much against the grain, he is forced to become a borrower. He is inclined to be thrifty but does not succeed in saving more than £300 until he is past fifty, and rejoices in the thought that henceforward he will be 'entitled annually to £9'. The labour of 'hopelessly endeavouring to get in subscriptions' for one of his books, is so great that 'I abhor the sight of a pen, and if I were an angel I would immediately moult all my quills for fear of their being used in calligraphy'. He dislikes the financial aspect of his work, but in spite of a large circle of friends and acquaintances and growing reputation both as artist and humorist, the task of earning a living remains a problem and a cause of anxiety. He has long been an artistic lion, one of the 'sights' of Cannes, Valetta, Corfu—or where-ever he may have pitched his studio, but his numerous visitors seem more inclined to sponge on his personal charm than to buy his pictures, and he dislikes being lionised at any time. At Malta he was 'dubbed a mystery and a savage' because he fled from the crowd of visitors who would have thronged his rooms without dreaming of spending £5 on a drawing. In a whole season he 'only got £30 from the rich Cannes public'. He had a bad winter in 1878 at San Remo, having sold but one drawing for £7, and would have 'come to grief' had it not been for two friends who bought some of his smaller oil paintings. In addition to these fluctuations in turnover, he suffers from the failure of his publisher, and his troubles are increased when the tenants of his villa at San Remo abscond owing him nearly £100.

11

He broods less upon these material worries than upon the evanescence of life and of all those things, friendship and the beauty of the earth, which are his real attachments. He is capable of consoling himself for the shortage of material possessions with a quip, but his acute sense of the shortage of time is not so easily assuaged. He attempts to soothe his temporal anxieties by resort to those apologetics which are common to all who are sensitive to evanescence. 'The fact is,' he argues, 'time is all nonsense,' and he inclines to leave it at that, resolving the incomprehensible by invincible pursuit of his chosen craft. His pictures give permanence to memories and impression and thus create a desirable illusion of timelessness. Yet the possession of a keen sense of fact will not permit him to be more than temporarily soothed by such arguments. He cannot bluff himself. He knows he is walking in the 'dusty twilight of the incomprehensible' and instinctively seeks to escape through the door of nonsense. 'I wish I were an egg and going to be hatched,' he sighs, summing up his desire for Nirvana.

12

Lear's nonsense is no mere tissue of quips and jokes. It is a thing in itself in a world of its own, with its own physiography and natural history; a world in which the nature of things has been changed, whilst retaining its own logical and consistent idiom. He expresses a nonsensical condition which is peculiar to himself and necessary to his serenity, and it may be that this fantastic world gratifies for him a desire which we all share to some extent, probably more than we are willing to admit, and which he seems to share, by anticipation, with the surrealists of our own time.

The authentic brand of nonsense is rarely absent from his letters, if no more than the fantastic spelling of a word. The art perfected in the *Nonsense Books* is here seen in the rough. It is not surprising, for instance, that the far-fetched hope of selling his Tennyson illustrations for the large sum of £18,000 should set him off. In that unlikely event, he will buy a 'chocolate coloured carriage speckled with gold, driven by a coachman in green vestments and silver spectacles wherein sitting on a lofty cushion composed of muffins and volumes of the Apocrypha', he will 'disport himself all about the London parks to the general satisfaction of all pious people, and the particular joy of Chichester, Lord Carlingford and his affectionate friend Edward Lear'. Here we have nonsense combined with humour, and there are many similar passages in the letters. In one of them he threatens to go to Darjeeling or Para and 'silently subsist on Parrot Pudding and Lizard Lozenges in chubbly contentment'. Lear is not a good sailor and once he writes from Folkestone that if the sea is rough he will hire, somewhat inconsistently, 'a pussilanimouse porpoise, and cross on his bak'. He records that one of his frequent coughs shakes off one of his toes, '2 teeth and 3 whiskers,' and he is so irritated by the doctor's concern that he orders 'a baked Barometer for dinner and 2 Thermometers stewed in treacle for supper'.

13

Lear is an adept at the game of monkeying with words. Like Rabelais and Swift and Joyce he has a genius for fantastic verbal adventures, but often they do little more than play tricks with established spelling. The more familiar the words the more he is tempted to tamper with them. The habit is ingrained, the result not alone of a natural love of the whimsical and an indomitable sense of fun, but it is also, as he himself is aware, an instinctive effort to bridge a gap between idea and expression. 'Proper and exact "epithets" always were impossible to me,' he says, 'as my thoughts are ever in advance of my words.' And here also we may discover a key to his nonsense, or 'nonsenses', as he calls them, which are perhaps ahead of rather than behind his senses.

In the first of his published letters to Fortescue, whom he likes to address as '40scue', he recounts the names of the distinguished foreigners at Rome, in 1848, as: 'Madame Pul-itz-neck-off and Count Bigenouf—Baron Polysuky, and Mons. Pig.' He is afraid to stand near the door, lest the announced names should make him grin. In his letters as well as his books he rattles off strings of queer examples with familiar gusto. A projected journey to Egypt makes him 'quite crazy about Memphis and On and Isis and crocodiles and ophthalmia and nubians and simoons and sorcerers and sphingidos'.

It is natural that Lear should have fallen, as we should now believe, into the then widespread vogue of punning. But he is no slavish imitator of Lamb and Hood. Even his puns have a style of their own which often trips over the boundaries of humour into his own rightful realm of nonsense. Here is an example from a letter of 1865:

'This place (Nice) is so wonderfully dry that nothing can be kept moist. I never was in so dry a place in all my life. When the little children cry, they cry dust and not tears. There is some water in the sea, but not much:—all the wet nurses cease to be so immediately on arriving:—Dryden is the only book read—the neighbourhood abounds with Dryads and Hammer-dryads: and weterinary surgeons are quite unknown.'

A trip to the Ionian Islands induced a punning declension of archipelago: 'v.a. Archipelago, P. Archipelament, P.P. Archipelagore.' In the same manner he has 'German, Gerwomen and Gerchildren', and such constructions as 'geraffino' for a young Giraffe, and 'hippopotamice' as an improved plural for hippopotamus.

Elsewhere he performs a different trick with an undertone of Learian irony:

'I went into the city to-day; to put the £125 I got for the 'Book of Nonsense' into the funds. It is doubtless a very unusual thing for an artist to put by money, for the whole way from Temple Bar to the Bank was *crowded* with carriages and people—so immense a sensation did this occurrence make. And all the way back it was the same, which was very gratifying.'

14

But as he is not content with being a punster, he quickly enters into the fun of any verbal trick new or old, and when Charles Dickens popularises Wellerisms, Lear becomes an easy convert to that once fashionable kind of humour: 'On the whole, as the morbid and mucilaginous monkey said when he climbed up to the top of the Palm-tree and found no fruit there, one can't depend upon dates.' The vocabulary of Sam Weller is also exploited in 'viddy' for 'widow', and 'wurbl' for 'verbal', and among other Cockneyisms such mispronunciations as 'chimbly' (chimney) and 'suddingly', recall Mrs. Gamp.

Phonetic spelling plays a considerable part in many of his nonsense words, and often a complete effect is obtained by this process as in 'yott' (yacht), 'rox' (rocks), 'korn' (corn), and 'toppix' (topics). He is better, however, in distortions like 'buzzim' (bosom), 'omejutly' (immediately), 'pollygise' (apologise), 'spongetaneous (spontaneous), 'mewtshool' (mutual), 'gnoat' (note), 'fizzicle' (physical), 'fizziognomy' (physiognomy), and 'phibs' (fibs).

He weds the 'n' or 'an' with the next word, as 'a narmchair', 'a nemptystummuk', 'a noppertunity', 'sill kankerchief', and indulges in the superfluous aspirate, as 'hempty'. Sometimes he translates whole sentences into nonsense-spelling, as 'I gnoo how bizzy u were', or 'witch fax I only came at granuously', or 'phits of coffin' or 'sombod a nokking at the dolorous door', or 'vorx of hart', and reports that he has 'become like a sparry in the pilderpips and a pemmican on the housetops', which reads like an excerpt from *Finnegans Wake!* He likes an absurdity such as 'sufficient unto the day is the weevil thereof', and in 'Mary Squeen of Cots' he anticipates the verbal inversion known later as a Spoonerism. The fun reaches a climax when inflation is added to distortion and his imagination bodies forth a portmanteau-word of no less than thirty-one letters like *splendidophorophero-stiphongious*, to express his satisfaction with a dinner-party.

It is none of these verbal adventures, however, that reveal Edward Lear at his best as a word-maker. In the examples I have given he is doing little more than amusing himself and his friends by following a fashion of the moment for that sort of thing, although his success indicates both a natural gift for word-building and a need for that kind of expression. His inventiveness is extraordinary and what nearly always begins as fun often ends in an extension of the boundaries of expression. His imagination is always at its best when it has some concrete form or idea for its objective. This is proved by the nomenclature of his nonsense creatures. In this realm he has only one peer—Lewis Carroll. But where the creator of *Alice* has some half dozen masterpieces to his credit such as the *Jabberwock*, *Bandersnatch*, *Snark* and *Boojum*, Lear has a whole zooful of distinguished creatures many of which, like the *Pobble* and the *Quangle Wangle*, have become common objects of the popular imagination.

15

This busy and distracted man wrote and illustrated, or illustrated for others, a score of volumes, and left in manuscript many more, including diaries, letters and, as he called them, 'nonsenses'. In addition, his landscapes in oil and water-colours, his realistic representations of parrots and other creatures, and his masterly nonsense drawings in black-and-white, which often anticipate Phil May's style and economy of line, would fill a fair-sized gallery; and he had some considerable fame among his large circle of friends as a composer of songs, particularly with Tennyson's words, which he would render with great expression in a thin tenor voice, often reducing his select audiences to tears.

16

This collection of the Nonsense of Edward Lear forms a complete reproduction of the four volumes of nonsense published during the author's lifetime, together with a few hitherto unpublished pieces included in the selection called *Nonsense Songs and Stories*, edited by Sir Edward Strachey, in 1895. In this collection there appeared for the first time the characteristic self-portrait in verse reproduced in the present volume.

I was at first tempted to re-arrange the various items in some sort of classification, but remembering that this collection is for entertainment I decided to follow the Lear tradition by arranging the sections in chronological order. The reader may thus roam about and pick and choose at will—which, after all, is the pleasantest way to know Mr. Lear. Another advantage of this method is that all the illustrations are placed where Lear intended them, and as integral to his art of nonsense. I have included specimens of his music and of his handwriting, and also a pictorial record of Old Foss, the cat, and on the title page an example of his epistolary caricatures of himself from an autograph in my possession.

The early nonsense books are not readily accessible as most of them were very properly used up, or eaten up, by the children for whom they were written. The original editions of *The Book of Nonsense* (1846), as well as *Nonsense Songs, Stories, Botany and Alphabets* (1871), *More Nonsense* (1872) and *Laughable Lyrics* (1877), are all scarce. It is easier to find a *First Folio Shakespeare* than a first edition of *The Book of Nonsense*: even the British Museum Library has to content itself with a copy of the third edition (1861). The popularity of that book has been continuous and progressive for a hundred years. During the author's lifetime there were many editions, and scarcely a year has since passed without a reprint.

I am obliged to Mr. George Macy of New York for the courtesy of permission to use as the basis of this Introduction the study of Edward Lear written originally for his bibliographical review, *The Dolphin*, and I am indebted to the following sources for biographical details: The *Letters of Edward Lear* (1907) and *Late Letters of Edward Lear* (1911), both edited by Lady Strachey; Mr. Angus Davidson's *Edward Lear: Landscape Painter and Nonsense Poet* (1938); and *Edward Lear on My Shelves*, the monumental folio by which Mr. William B. Osgood Field, the distinguished American bibliophile, has celebrated Edward Lear and his own unique collection of Lear manuscripts and first editions.

I

A BOOK OF NONSENSE
(1846)

There was an Old Man with a beard,
Who said, 'It is just as I feared!—
Two Owls and a Hen, four Larks and a Wren,
Have all built their nests in my beard!'

There was a Young Lady of Ryde,
Whose shoe-strings were seldom untied;
She purchased some clogs, and some small spotty dogs,
And frequently walked about Ryde.

There was an Old Man with a nose,
Who said, 'If you choose to suppose,
That my nose is too long, you are certainly wrong!'
That remarkable Man with a nose.

There was an Old Man on a hill,
Who seldom, if ever, stood still;
He ran up and down, in his Grandmother's gown,
Which adorned that Old Man on a hill.

There was a Young Lady whose bonnet,
Came untied when the birds sate upon it;
But she said, 'I don't care! all the birds in the air
Are welcome to sit on my bonnet!'

There was a Young Person of Smyrna,
Whose Grandmother threatened to burn her;
But she seized on the Cat, and said, 'Granny, burn that!
You incongruous Old Woman of Smyrna!'

There was an Old Person of Chili,
Whose conduct was painful and silly,
He sate on the stairs, eating apples and pears,
That imprudent Old Person of Chili.

There was an Old Man with a gong,
Who bumped at it all the day long;
But they called out, 'O law! you're a horrid old bore!'
So they smashed that Old Man with a gong.

6

There was an Old Lady of Chertsey,
Who made a remarkable curtsey;
She twirled round and round, till she sunk underground,
Which distressed all the people of Chertsey.

There was an Old Man in a tree,
Who was horribly bored by a Bee;
When they said, 'Does it buzz?' he replied, 'Yes, it does!'
'It's a regular brute of a Bee!'

There was an Old Man with a flute,
A sarpint ran into his boot;
But he played day and night, till the sarpint took flight,
And avoided that man with a flute.

There was a Young Lady whose chin,
Resembled the point of a pin;
So she had it made sharp, and purchased a harp,
And played several tunes with her chin.

There was an Old Man of Kilkenny,
Who never had more than a penny;
He spent all that money, in onions and honey,
That wayward Old Man of Kilkenny.

There was an Old Person of Ischia,
Whose conduct grew friskier and friskier;
He danced hornpipes and jigs, and ate thousands of figs,
That lively old Person of Ischia.

9

There was an Old Man in a boat,
Who said, 'I'm afloat! I'm afloat!'
When they said, 'No! you ain't!' he was ready to faint,
That unhappy Old Man in a boat.

There was a Young Lady of Portugal,
Whose ideas were excessively nautical:
She climbed up a tree, to examine the sea,
But declared she would never leave Portugal.

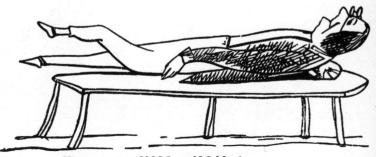

There was an Old Man of Moldavia,
Who had the most curious behaviour;
For while he was able, he slept on a table.
That funny Old Man of Moldavia.

There was an Old Man of Madras,
Who rode on a cream-coloured ass;
But the length of its ears, so promoted his fears,
That it killed that Old Man of Madras.

There was an Old Person of Leeds,
Whose head was infested with beads;
She sat on a stool, and ate gooseberry fool,
Which agreed with that person of Leeds.

There was an Old Man of Peru,
Who never knew what he should do;
So he tore off his hair, and behaved like a bear,
That intrinsic Old Man of Peru.

There was an Old Person of Hurst,
Who drank when he was not athirst;
When they said, 'You'll grow fatter,' he answered, 'What matter?'
That globular Person of Hurst.

There was a Young Person of Crete,
Whose toilette was far from complete;
She dressed in a sack, spickle-speckled with black,
That ombliferous person of Crete.

There was an Old Man of the Isles,
Whose face was pervaded with smiles:
He sung high dum diddle, and played on the fiddle,
That amiable Man of the Isles.

There was an Old Person of Buda,
Whose conduct grew ruder and ruder;
Till at last, with a hammer, they silenced his clamour,
By smashing that Person of Buda.

There was an Old Man of Columbia,
Who was thirsty, and called out for some beer;
But they brought it quite hot, in a small copper pot,
Which disgusted that man of Columbia.

There was a Young Lady of Dorking,
Who bought a large bonnet for walking;
But its colour and size, so bedazzled her eyes,
That she very soon went back to Dorking.

There was an Old Man who supposed,
That the street door was partially closed;
But some very large rats, ate his coats and his hats,
While that futile old gentleman dozed.

There was an Old Man of the West,
Who wore a pale plum-coloured vest;
When they said, 'Does it fit?' he replied, 'Not a bit!'
That uneasy Old Man of the West.

16

There was an Old Man of the Wrekin
Whose shoes made a horrible creaking
But they said 'Tell us whether, your shoes are of leather,
Or of what, you Old Man of the Wrekin?'

There was a Young Lady whose eyes,
Were unique as to colour and size;
When she opened them wide, people all turned aside,
And started away in surprise.

There was a Young Lady of Norway,
Who casually sat in a doorway;
When the door squeezed her flat, she exclaimed 'What of that?'
This courageous Young Lady of Norway.

There was an Old Man of Vienna,
Who lived upon Tincture of Senna;
When that did not agree, he took Camomile Tea,
That nasty Old Man of Vienna.

18

There was an old Person whose habits,
Induced him to feed upon Rabbits;
When he'd eaten eighteen, he turned perfectly green,
Upon which he relinquished those habits.

There was an old person of Dover,
Who rushed through a field of blue Clover;
But some very large bees, stung his nose and his knees,
So he very soon went back to Dover.

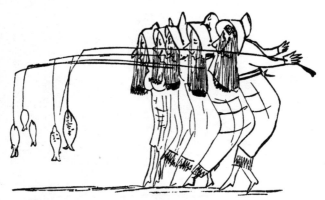

There was an Old Man of Marseilles,
Whose daughters wore bottle-green veils;
They caught several Fish, which they put in a dish,
And sent to their Pa' at Marseilles.

There was an Old Person of Cadiz,
Who was always polite to all ladies;
But in handing his daughter, he fell into the water,
Which drowned that Old Person of Cadiz.

20

There was an Old Person of Basing,
Whose presence of mind was amazing;
He purchased a steed, which he rode at full speed,
And escaped from the people of Basing.

There was an old Man of Quebec,
A beetle ran over his neck;
But he cried, 'With a needle, I'll slay you, O beadle!'
That angry Old Man of Quebec.

There was an Old Person of Philœ,
Whose conduct was scroobious and wily;
He rushed up a Palm, when the weather was calm,
And observed all the ruins of Philœ.

There was a Young Lady of Bute,
Who played on a silver-gilt flute;
She played several jigs, to her uncle's white pigs,
That amusing Young Lady of Bute.

There was a Young Lady whose nose,
Was so long that it reached to her toes;
So she hired an Old Lady, whose conduct was steady,
To carry that wonderful nose.

There was a Young Lady of Turkey,
Who wept when the weather was murky;
When the day turned out fine, she ceased to repine,
That capricious Young Lady of Turkey.

There was an Old Man of Apulia,
Whose conduct was very peculiar
He fed twenty sons, upon nothing but buns,
That whimsical Man of Apulia,

There was an Old Man with a poker,
Who painted his face with red oker
When they said, 'You're a Guy!' he made no reply,
But knocked them all down with his poker.

There was an Old Person of Prague,
Who was suddenly seized with the plague;
But they gave him some butter, which caused him to mutter,
And cured that Old Person of Prague.

There was an Old Man of the North,
Who fell into a basin of broth;
But a laudable cook, fished him out with a hook,
Which saved that Old Man of the North.

There was a Young Lady of Poole,
Whose soup was excessively cool;
So she put it to boil by the aid of some oil,
That ingenious Young Lady of Poole.

There was an Old Person of Mold,
Who shrank from sensations of cold;
So he purchased some muffs, some furs and some fluffs,
And wrapped himself from the cold.

There was an Old Man of Nepaul,
From his horse had a terrible fall;
But, though split quite in two, by some very strong glue,
They mended that Man of Nepaul.

There was an old Man of th' Abruzzi,
So blind that he couldn't his foot see;
When they said, 'That's your toe,' he replied, 'Is it so?'
That doubtful old Man of th' Abruzzi.

There was an Old Person of Rhodes,
Who strongly objected to toads;
He paid several cousins, to catch them by dozens,
That futile Old Person of Rhodes.

There was an Old Man of Peru,
Who watched his wife making a stew;
But once by mistake, in a stove she did bake,
That unfortunate Man of Peru.

There was an Old Man of Melrose,
Who walked on the tips of his toes;
But they said, 'It ain't pleasant, to see you at present,
You stupid Old Man of Melrose.'

There was a Young Lady of Lucca,
Whose lovers completely forsook her;
She ran up a tree, and said, 'Fiddle-de-dee!'
Which embarassed the people of Lucca.

There was an old Man of Bohemia,
Whose daughter was christened Euphemia;
Till one day, to his grief, she married a thief,
Which grieved that old Man of Bohemia.

There was an Old Man of Vesuvius,
Who studied the works of Vitruvius;
When the flames burnt his book, to drinking he took,
That morbid Old Man of Vesuvius.

There was an Old Man of Cape Horn,
Who wished he had never been born;
So he sat on a chair, till he died of despair,
That dolorous Man of Cape Horn.

There was an Old Lady whose folly,
Induced her to sit in a holly;
Whereon by a thorn, her dress being torn,
She quickly became melancholy.

There was an Old Man of Corfu,
Who never knew what he should do;
So he rushed up and down, till the sun made him brown,
That bewildered Old Man of Corfu.

There was an Old Man of the South,
Who had an immoderate mouth;
But in swallowing a dish, that was quite full of fish,
He was choked, that Old Man of the South.

There was an Old Man of the Nile,
Who sharpened his nails with a file;
Till he cut off his thumbs, and said calmly, 'This comes—
Of sharpening one's nails with a file!'

There was an Old Person of Rheims,
Who was troubled with horrible dreams;
So, to keep him awake, they fed him with cake.
Which amused that Old Person of Rheims.

There was an Old Person of Cromer,
Who stood on one leg to read Homer;
When he found he grew stiff, he jumped over the cliff,
Which concluded that Person of Cromer.

There was an Old Person of Troy,
Whose drink was warm brandy and soy;
Which he took with a spoon, by the light of the moon,
In sight of the city of Troy.

There was an Old Man of the Dee,
Who was sadly annoyed by a flea;
When he said, 'I will scratch it'—they gave him a hatchet,
Which grieved that Old Man of the Dee.

There was an Old Man of Dundee,
Who frequented the top of a tree;
When disturbed by the crows, he abruptly arose,
And exclaimed, 'I'll return to Dundee.'

There was an Old Person of Tring,
Who embellished his nose with a ring;
He gazed at the moon, every evening in June,
That ecstatic Old Person of Tring.

There was an Old Man on some rocks,
Who shut his wife up in a box,
When she said, 'Let me out,' he exclaimed, 'Without doubt,
You will pass all your life in that box.'

There was an Old Man of Coblenz,
The length of whose legs was immense;
He went with one prance, from Turkey to France,
That surprising Old Man of Coblenz.

There was an Old Man of Calcutta,
Who perpetually ate bread and butter;
Till a great bit of muffin, on which he was stuffing,
Choked that horrid old man of Calcutta.

There was an Old Man in a pew,
Whose waistcoat was spotted with blue;
But he tore it in pieces, to give to his nieces,—
That cheerful Old Man in a pew.

There was an Old Man who said,
'How,—shall I flee from this horrible Cow?
I will sit on this stile, and continue to smile,
Which may soften the heart of that Cow.'

There was a Young Lady of Hull,
Who was chased by a virulent Bull;
But she seized on a spade, and called out—'Who's **afraid**!'
Which distracted that virulent Bull.

There was an Old Man of Whitehaven,
Who danced a quadrille with a Raven;
But they said—'It's absurd, to encourage this bird!'
So they smashed that Old Man of Whitehaven.

There was an Old Man of Leghorn,
The smallest as ever was born;
But quickly snapt up he, was once by a puppy,
Who devoured that Old Man of Leghorn.

There was an old Man of the Hague,
Whose ideas were excessively vague;
He built a balloon, to examine the moon,
That deluded Old Man of the Hague.

There was an Old Man of Jamaica,
Who suddenly married a Quaker!
But she cried out—'O lack! I have married a black!'
Which distressed that Old Man of Jamaica.

There was an old person of Dutton,
Whose head was so small as a button:
So to make it look big, he purchased a wig,
And rapidly rushed about Dutton.

There was a young Lady of Tyre,
Who swept the loud chords of a lyre;
At the sound of each sweep, she enraptured the deep,
And enchanted the city of Tyre.

There was an Old Man who said, 'Hush!
I perceive a young bird in this bush!'
When they said—'Is it small?' He replied—'Not at all!
It is four times as big as the bush!'

There was an Old Man of the East,
Who gave all his children a feast;
But they all eat so much, and their conduct was such,
That it killed that Old Man of the East.

There was an Old Man of Kamschatka,
Who possessed a remarkably fat cur.
His gait and his waddle, were held as a model,
To all the fat dogs in Kamschatka.

There was an Old Man of the Coast,
Who placidly sat on a post;
But when it was cold, he relinquished his hold,
And called for some hot buttered toast.

There was an Old Person of Bangor,
Whose face was distorted with anger,
He tore off his boots, and subsisted on roots,
That borascible person of Bangor.

44

There was an Old Man with a beard,
Who sat on a horse when he reared;
But they said, 'Never mind! you will fall off behind,
You propitious Old Man with a beard!'

There was an Old Man of the West,
Who never could get any rest;
So they set him to spin, on his nose and his chin,
Which cured that Old Man of the West.

There was an Old Person of Anerley,
Whose conduct was strange and unmannerly;
He rushed down the Strand, with a Pig in each hand,
But returned in the evening to Anerley.

There was a Young Lady of Troy,
Whom several large flies did annoy;
Some she killed with a thump, some she drowned at the pump,
And some she took with her to Troy.

There was an Old Man of Berlin,
Whose form was uncommonly thin;
Till he once, by mistake, was mixed up in a cake,
So they baked that Old Man of Berlin.

There was an Old Person of Spain,
Who hated all trouble and pain;
So he sate on a chair, with his feet in the air,
That umbrageous Old Person of Spain.

47

There was a Young Lady of Russia,
Who screamed so that no one could hush her;
Her screams were extreme, no one heard such a scream,
As was screamed by that Lady of Russia.

There was an Old Man who said, 'Well!
Will *nobody* answer this bell?
I have pulled day and night, till my hair has grown white,
But nobody answers this bell!'

There was a Young Lady of Wales,
Who caught a large fish without scales;
When she lifted her hook, she exclaimed, 'Only look!'
That extatic Young Lady of Wales.

There was an Old Person of Cheadle,
Was put in the stocks by the beadle;
For stealing some pigs, some coats and some wigs,
That horrible Person of Cheadle.

There was a Young Lady of Welling,
Whose praise all the world was a telling;
She played on the harp, and caught several carp,
That accomplished Young Lady of Welling.

There was an Old Person of Tartary,
Who divided his jugular artery;
But he screeched to his wife, and she said, 'Oh, my life!
Your death will be felt by all Tartary!'

There was an old Person of Chester,
Whom several small children did pester;
They threw some large stones, which broke most of his bones,
And displeased that old person of Chester.

There was an Old Man with an owl,
Who continued to bother and howl;
He sate on a rail, and imbibed bitter ale,
Which refreshed that Old Man and his owl.

There was an Old Person of Gretna,
Who rushed down the crater of Etna;
When they said, 'Is it hot?' He replied, 'No, it's not!'
That mendacious Old Person of Gretna.

There was a Young Lady of Sweden,
Who went by the slow train to Weedon;
When they cried, 'Weedon Station!' she made no observation,
But she thought she should go back to Sweden.

There was a Young Girl of Majorca,
Whose aunt was a very fast walker;
She walked seventy miles, and leaped fifteen stiles,
Which astonished that Girl of Majorca.

There was an Old Man of the Cape,
Who possessed a large Barbary Ape;
Till the Ape one dark night, set the house on a light,
Which burned that Old Man of the Cape.

There was an Old Lady of Prague,
Whose language was horribly vague.
When they said, 'Are these caps?' she answered, 'Perhaps!'
That oracular Lady of Prague.

There was an Old Person of Sparta,
Who had twenty-five sons and one daughter;
He fed them on snails, and weighed them in scales,
That wonderful person of Sparta.

There was an Old Man at a casement,
Who held up his hands in amazement;
When they said, 'Sir! you'll fall!' he replied, 'Not at all!'
That incipient Old Man at a casement.

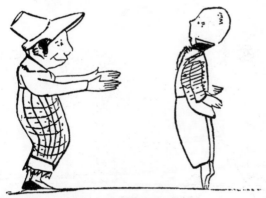

There was an old Person of Burton,
Whose answers were rather uncertain;
When they said, 'How d'ye do?' he replied, 'Who are you?'
That distressing old person of Burton.

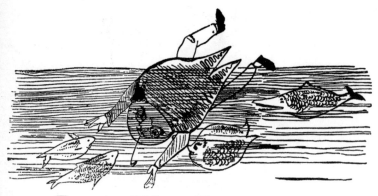

There was an Old Person of Ems,
Who casually fell in the Thames;
And when he was found, they said he was drowned,
That unlucky Old Person of Ems.

There was an Old Person of Ewell,
Who chiefly subsisted on gruel;
But to make it more nice, he inserted some mice,
Which refreshed that Old Person of Ewell.

There was a Young Lady of Parma,
Whose conduct grew calmer and calmer;
When they said, 'Are you dumb?' she merely said, 'Hum!'
That provoking Young Lady of Parma.

There was an Old Man of Aôsta,
Who possessed a large Cow, but he lost her;
But they said, 'Don't you see, she has rushed up a tree?
You invidious Old Man of Aôsta!'

There was an Old Man, on whose nose,
Most birds of the air could repose;
But they all flew away, at the closing of day,
Which relieved that Old Man and his nose.

There was a Young Lady of Clare,
Who was sadly pursued by a bear;
When she found she was tired, she abruptly expired,
That unfortunate Lady of Clare.

II

NONSENSE SONGS,
STORIES   BOTANY
AND
ALPHABETS
(1871)

NONSENSE SONGS

THE OWL AND THE PUSSY-CAT

I

The Owl and the Pussy-cat went to sea
   In a beautiful pea-green boat,
They took some honey, and plenty of money,
   Wrapped up in a five-pound note.
The Owl looked up to the stars above,
   And sang to a small guitar,
'O lovely Pussy! O Pussy, my love,
     What a beautiful Pussy you are,
        You are,
        You are!
   What a beautiful Pussy you are!'

II

Pussy said to the Owl, 'You elegant fowl!
　　How charmingly sweet you sing!
O let us be married! too long we have tarried:
　　But what shall we do for a ring?'
They sailed away, for a year and a day,
　　To the land where the Bong-tree grows
And there in a wood a Piggy-wig stood
　　With a ring at the end of his nose,
　　　　His nose,
　　　　His nose,
　　With a ring at the end of his nose.

III

'Dear Pig, are you willing to sell for one shilling
　　Your ring?' Said the Piggy, 'I will.'
So they took it away, and were married next day
　　By the Turkey who lives on the hill.
They dined on mince, and slices of quince,
　　Which they ate with a runcible spoon;

And hand in hand, on the edge of the sand,
  They danced by the light of the moon,
      The moon,
      The moon,
They danced by the light of the moon.

THE DUCK AND THE KANGAROO

I

Said the Duck to the Kangaroo,
  'Good gracious! how you hop!
Over the fields and the water too,
  As if you never would stop!
My life is a bore in this nasty pond,
And I long to go out in the world beyond!
    I wish I could hop like you!'
    Said the Duck to the Kangaroo.

II

'Please give me a ride on your back!'
    Said the Duck to the Kangaroo.
'I would sit quite still, and say nothing but "Quack,"
    The whole of the long day through!
And we'd go to the Dee, and the Jelly Bo Lee,
Over the land, and over the sea;—
    Please take me a ride! O do!'
    Said the Duck to the Kangaroo.

III

Said the Kangaroo to the Duck,
   'This requires some little reflection;
Perhaps on the whole it might bring me luck,
   And there seems but one objection,
Which is, if you'll let me speak so bold,
Your feet are unpleasantly wet and cold,
And would probably give me the roo-
   Matiz!' said the Kangaroo.

IV

Said the Duck, 'As I sate on the rocks,
  I have thought over that completely,
And I bought four pairs of worsted socks
  Which fit my web-feet neatly.
And to keep out the cold I've bought a cloak,
And every day a cigar I'll smoke,
  All to follow my own dear true
  Love of a Kangaroo!'

V

Said the Kangaroo, 'I'm ready!
  All in the moonlight pale;
But to balance me well, dear Duck, sit steady!
  And quite at the end of my tail!'
So away they went with a hop and a bound,
And they hopped the whole world three times round;
  And who so happy,—O who,
  As the Duck and the Kangaroo?

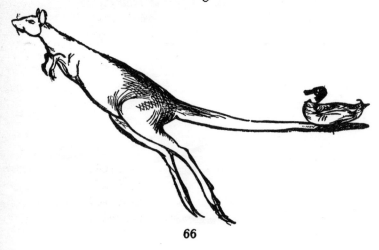

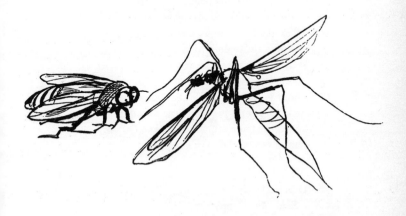

THE DADDY LONG-LEGS AND THE FLY

I

Once Mr. Daddy Long-legs,
   Dressed in brown and gray,
Walked about upon the sands
   Upon a summer's day;
And there among the pebbles,
   When the wind was rather cold,
He met with Mr. Floppy Fly,
   All dressed in blue and gold.
And as it was too soon to dine,
They drank some Periwinkle-wine,
And played an hour or two, or more,
At battlecock and shuttledore.

Said Mr. Daddy Long-legs
   To Mr. Floppy Fly,
'Why do you never come to court?
   I wish you'd tell me why.
All gold and shine, in dress so fine,
   You'd quite delight the court.
Why do you never go at all?
   I really think you *ought!*
And if you went, you'd see such sights!
Such rugs! and jugs! and candle-lights!
And more than all, the King and Queen,
One in red, and one in green!'

'O Mr. Daddy Long-legs,'
   Said Mr. Floppy Fly,
'It's true I never go to court,
   And I will tell you why.
If I had six long legs like yours,
   At once I'd go to court!
But oh! I can't, because *my* legs
   Are so extremely short.
And I'm afraid the King and Queen
(One in red, and one in green)
Would say aloud, "You are not fit,
You Fly, to come to court a bit!"

'O Mr. Daddy Long-Legs,'
   Said Mr. Floppy Fly,
'I wish you'd sing one little song!
   One mumbian melody!

68

You used to sing so awful well
   In former days gone by,
But now you never sing at all;
   I wish you'd tell me why:
For if you would, the silvery sound
Would please the shrimps and cockles round,
And all the crabs would gladly come
To hear you sing, "Ah, Hum di Hum"!'

V

Said Mr. Daddy Long-legs,
   'I can never sing again!
And if you wish, I'll tell you why,
   Although it gives me pain.
For years I cannot hum a bit,
   Or sing the smallest song;
And this the dreadful reason is,
   My legs are grown too long!
My six long legs, all here and there,
Oppress my bosom with despair;
And if I stand, or lie, or sit,
I cannot sing one single bit!'

VI

So Mr. Daddy Long-legs
   And Mr. Floppy Fly
Sat down in silence by the sea,
   And gazed upon the sky.
They said, 'This is a dreadful thing!
The world has all gone wrong,
Since one has legs too short by half,
   The other much too long!

One never more can go to court,
Because his legs have grown too short;
The other cannot sing a song,
Because his legs have grown too long!'

VII

Then Mr. Daddy Long-legs
    And Mr. Floppy Fly
Rushed downward to the foamy sea
    With one sponge-taneous cry;
And there they found a little boat,
    Whose sails were pink and gray;
And off they sailed among the waves,
    Far, and far away.
They sailed across the silent main,
And reached the great Gromboolian plain;
And there they play for evermore
At battlecock and shuttledoor.

THE JUMBLIES

I

They went to sea in a Sieve, they did,
  In a Sieve they went to sea:
In spite of all their friends could say,
On a winter's morn, on a stormy day,
  In a Sieve they went to sea!
And when the Sieve turned round and round,
And every one cried, 'You'll all be drowned!'
They called aloud, 'Our Sieve ain't big,
But we don't care a button! we don't care a fig!
  In a Sieve we'll go to sea!'
    Far and few, far and few,
      Are the lands where the Jumblies live;
      Their heads are green, and their hands are blue,
        And they went to sea in a Sieve.

II

They sailed away in a Sieve, they did,
  In a Sieve they sailed so fast,
With only a beautiful pea-green veil
Tied with a riband by way of a sail,
  To a small tobacco-pipe mast;
And every one said, who saw them go,
'O won't they be soon upset, you know!
For the sky is dark, and the voyage is long,
And happen what may, it's extremely wrong
  In a Sieve to sail so fast!'
    Far and few, far and few,
      Are the lands where the Jumblies live;
      Their heads are green, and their hands are blue,
        And they went to sea in a Sieve.

III

The water it soon came in, it did,
  The water it soon came in;
So to keep them dry, they wrapped their feet
In a pinky paper all folded neat,
  And they fastened it down with a pin.
And they passed the night in a crockery-jar,
And each of them said, 'How wise we are!
Though the sky be dark, and the voyage be long,
Yet we never can think we were rash or wrong,
  While round in our Sieve we spin!'
    Far and few, far and few,
      Are the lands where the Jumblies live;
      Their heads are green, and their hands are blue,
        And they went to sea in a Sieve.

IV

And all night long they sailed away;
   And when the sun went down,
They whistled and warbled a moony song
To the echoing sound of a coppery gong,
   In the shade of the mountains brown.
'O Timballo! How happy we are,
When we live in a sieve and a crockery-jar,
And all night long in the moonlight pale,
We sail away with a pea-green sail,
   In the shade of the mountains brown!'
     Far and few, far and few,
       Are the lands where the Jumblies live;
       Their heads are green, and their hands are blue,
       And they went to sea in a Sieve.

V

They sailed to the Western Sea, they did,
   To a land all covered with trees,
And they bought an Owl, and a useful Cart,
And a pound of Rice, and a Cranberry Tart,
   And a hive of silvery Bees.
And they bought a Pig, and some green Jack-daws,
And a lovely Monkey with lollipop paws,
And forty bottles of Ring-Bo-Ree,
   And no end of Stilton Cheese.
     Far and few, far and few,
       Are the lands where the Jumblies live;
       Their heads are green, and their hands are blue,
       And they went to sea in a Sieve.

And in twenty years they all came back,
  In twenty years or more,
And every one said, 'How tall they've grown!
For they've been to the Lakes, and the Torrible Zone,
  And the hills of the Chankly Bore;
And they drank their health, and gave them a feast
Of dumplings made of beautiful yeast;
And every one said, 'If we only live,
We too will go to sea in a Sieve,—
  To the hills of the Chankly Bore!'
    Far and few, far and few,
      Are the lands where the Jumblies live;
      Their heads are green, and their hands are blue,
        And they went to sea in a Sieve.

THE NUTCRACKERS AND THE
SUGAR-TONGS

I

The Nutcrackers sate by a plate on the table,
  The Sugar-tongs sate by a plate at his side;
And the Nutcrackers said, 'Don't you wish we were able
  'Along the blue hills and green meadows to ride?
'Must we drag on this stupid existence for ever,
  'So idle and weary, so full of remorse,—
'While every one else takes his pleasure, and never
  'Seems happy unless he is riding a horse?

II

'Don't you think we could ride without being instructed?
  'Without any saddle, or bridle, or spur?
'Our legs are so long, and so aptly constructed,
  'I'm sure that an accident could not occur.
'Let us all of a sudden hop down from the table,
  'And hustle downstairs, and each jump on a horse!
'Shall we try? Shall we go? Do you think we are able?'
  The Sugar-tongs answered distinctly, 'Of course!'

So down the long staircase they hopped in a minute,
  The Sugar-tongs snapped, and the Crackers said 'crack!'
The stable was open, the horses were in it;
  Each took out a pony, and jumped on his back.
The Cat in a fright scrambled out of the doorway,
  The Mice tumbled out of a bundle of hay,
The brown and white Rats, and the black ones from Norway,
  Screamed out, 'They are taking the horses away!'

IV

The whole of the household was filled with amazement,
  The Cups and the Saucers danced madly about,
The Plates and the Dishes looked out of the casement,
  The Saltcellar stood on his head with a shout,
The Spoons with a clatter looked out of the lattice,
  The Mustard-pot climbed up the Gooseberry Pies,
The Soup-ladle peeped through a heap of Veal Patties,
  And squeaked with a ladle-like scream of surprise.

V

The Frying-pan said, 'It's an awful delusion!'
  The Tea-kettle hissed and grew black in the face;
And they all rushed downstairs in the wildest confusion,
  To see the great Nutcracker-Sugar-tong race.
And out of the stable, with screamings and laughter,
  (Their ponies were cream-coloured, speckled with brown,)
The Nutcrackers first, and the Sugar-tongs after,
  Rode all round the yard, and then all round the town.

VI

They rode through the street, and they rode by the station,
  They galloped away to the beautiful shore;

In silence they rode, and 'made no observation',
  Save this: 'We will never go back any more!'
And still you might hear, till they rode out of hearing,
  The Sugar-tongs snap, and the Crackers say 'crack!'
Till far in the distance their forms disappearing,
  They faded away.—And they never came back!

CALICO PIE

I

Calico Pie,
The little Birds fly
Down to the calico tree,
  Their wings were blue,
  And they sang 'Tilly-loo!'
  Till away they flew,—
    And they never came back to me!
      They never came back!
      They never came back!
    They never came back to me!

II

  Calico Jam,
  The little Fish swam,
Over the syllabub sea,
      He took off his hat,

78

To the Sole and the Sprat,
And the Willeby-wat,—
But he never came back to me!

He never came back!
He never came back!
He never came back to me!

III

Calico Ban,
The little Mice ran,
To be ready in time for tea,
Flippity flup,
They drank it all up,
And danced in the cup,—

But they never came back to me!
They never came back!
They never came back!
They never came back to me!

iv

Calico Drum,
The Grasshoppers come,
The Butterfly, Beetle, and Bee,
Over the ground,
Around and round,
With a hop and a bound,—

But they never came back!
They never came back!
They never came back!
They never came back to me!

MR. AND MRS. SPIKKY SPARROW

I

On a little piece of wood,
Mr. Spikky Sparrow stood;
Mrs. Sparrow sate close by,
A-making of an insect pie,
For her little children five,
In the nest and all alive,
Singing with a cheerful smile
To amuse them all the while,
    Twikky wikky wikky wee,
    Wikky bikky twikky tee,
      Spikky bikky bee!

II

Mrs. Spikky Sparrow said,
'Spikky, Darling! in my head
'Many thoughts of trouble come,
'Like to flies upon a plum!
'All last night, among the trees,
'I heard you cough, I heard you sneeze;

'And, thought I, it's come to that
'Because he does not wear a hat!
   'Chippy wippy sikky tee!
   'Bikky wikky tikky mee!
     'Spikky chippy wee!

III

'Not that you are growing old,
'But the nights are growing cold.
'No one stays out all night long
'Without a hat: I'm sure it's wrong!'
Mr. Spikky said, 'How kind,
'Dear! you are, to speak your mind!
'All your life I wish you luck!
'You are! you are! a lovely duck!
   'Witchy witchy witchy wee!
   'Twitchy witchy witchy bee!
     'Tikky tikky tee!

IV

'I was also sad, and thinking,
'When one day I saw you winking,
'And I heard you sniffle-snuffle,
'And I saw your feathers ruffle;
'To myself I sadly said,
'She's neuralgia in her head!
'That dear head has nothing on it!
'Ought she not to wear a bonnet?
   'Witchy kitchy kitchy wee?
   'Spikky wikky mikky bee?
     'Chippy wippy chee?

82

'Let us both fly up to town!
'There I'll buy you such a gown!
'Which, completely in the fashion,
'You shall tie a sky-blue sash on.
'And a pair of slippers neat,
'To fit your darling little feet,
'So that you will look and feel
'Quite galloobious and genteel!
    'Jikky wikky bikky see,
    'Chicky bikky wikky bee,
        'Twicky witchy wee!'

VI

So they both to London went,
Alighting on the Monument,
Whence they flew down swiftly—pop,
Into Moses' wholesale shop;
There they bought a hat and bonnet,
And a gown with spots upon it,
A satin sash of Cloxam blue,
And a pair of slippers too.
    Zikky wikky mikky bee,
    Witchy witchy mitchy kee,
        Sikky tikky wee.

VII

Then when so completely drest,
Back they flew, and reached their nest.
Their children cried, 'O Ma and Pa!
'How truly beautiful you are!'
Said they, 'We trust that cold or pain

83

'We shall never feel again!
'While, perched on tree, or house, or steeple,
'We now shall look like other people.
    'Witchy witchy witchy wee,
    'Twikky mikky bikky bee,
        'Zikky sikky tee.'

THE BROOM, THE SHOVEL, THE POKER
AND THE TONGS

I

The Broom and the Shovel, the Poker and Tongs,
   They all took a drive in the Park,
And they each sang a song, Ding-a-dong, Ding-a-dong,
   Before they went back in the dark.
Mr. Poker he sate quite upright in the coach,
   Mr. Tongs made a clatter and clash,
Miss Shovel was dressed all in black (with a brooch),
   Mrs. Broom was in blue (with a sash).
      Ding-a-dong! Ding-a-dong!
      And they all sang a song!

II

'O Shovely so lovely!' the Poker he sang,
   'You have perfectly conquered my heart!
'Ding-a-dong! Ding-a-dong! If you're pleased with my song,
   'I will feed you with cold apple tart!
'When you scrape up the coals with a delicate sound,
   'You enrapture my life with delight!
'Your nose is so shiny! your head is so round!
   'And your shape is so slender and bright!
      'Ding-a-dong! Ding-a-dong!
      'Ain't you pleased with my song?'

III

'Alas! Mrs. Broom!' sighed the Tongs in his song,
  'O is it because I'm so thin,
'And my legs are so long—Ding-a-dong! Ding-a-dong!
  'That you don't care about me a pin?
'Ah! fairest of creatures, when sweeping the room,
  'Ah! why don't you heed my complaint!
'Must you needs be so cruel, you beautiful Broom,
  'Because you are covered with paint?
     'Ding-a-dong! Ding-a-dong!
     'You are certainly wrong!

IV

Mrs. Broom and Miss Shovel together they sang,
  'What nonsense you're singing to-day!'
Said the Shovel, 'I'll certainly hit you a bang!'
  Said the Broom, 'And I'll sweep you away!'
So the Coachman drove homeward as fast as he could,
  Perceiving their anger with pain;
But they put on the kettle, and little by little,
  They all became happy again.
     Ding-a-dong! Ding-a-dong!
     There's an end of my song!

THE TABLE AND THE CHAIR

I

Said the Table to the Chair,
'You can hardly be aware,
'How I suffer from the heat,
'And from chilblains on my feet!
'If we took a little walk,
'We might have a little talk!
'Pray let us take the air!'
Said the Table to the Chair.

II

Said the Chair unto the Table,
'Now you *know* we are not able!
'How foolishly you talk,
'When you know we *cannot* walk!'
Said the Table, with a sigh,

'It can do no harm to try,
'I've as many legs as you,
'Why can't we walk on two?'

III

So they both went slowly down,
And walked about the town
With a cheerful bumpy sound,
As they toddled round and round.
And everybody cried,
As they hastened to their side,
'See! the Table and the Chair
'Have come out to take the air!'

IV

But in going down an alley,
To a castle in a valley,
They completely lost their way,
And wandered all the day,

Till, to see them safely back,
They paid a Ducky-quack,
And a Beetle, and a Mouse,
Who took them to their house.

Then they whispered to each other,
'O delightful little brother!
'What a lovely walk we've taken!
'Let us dine on Beans and Bacon!'
So the Ducky, and the leetle
Browny-Mousy and the Beetle
Dined, and danced upon their heads
Till they toddled to their beds.

NONSENSE STORIES

THE STORY OF THE FOUR LITTLE CHILDREN WHO WENT ROUND THE WORLD

Once upon a time, a long while ago, there were four little people whose names were

VIOLET,   SLINGSBY,   GUY,   and LIONEL;

and they all thought they should like to see the world. So they bought a large boat to sail quite round the world by sea, and then they were to come back on the other side by land. The boat was painted blue with green spots, and the sail was yellow with red stripes; and when they set off, they only took a small Cat to steer and look after the boat, besides an elderly Quangle-Wangle, who had to cook the dinner and make the tea; for which purposes they took a large kettle.

91

For the first ten days they sailed on beautifully, and found plenty to eat, as there were lots of fish, and they had only to take them out of the sea with a long spoon, when the Quangle-Wangle instantly cooked them, and the Pussy-cat was fed with the bones, with which she expressed herself pleased on the whole, so that all the party were very happy.

During the day-time, Violet chiefly occupied herself in putting salt-water into a churn, while her three brothers churned it violently, in the hope that it would turn into butter, which it seldom, if ever did; and in the evening they all retired into the Tea-kettle, where they all managed to sleep very comfortably, while Pussy and the Quangle-Wangle managed the boat.

After a time they saw some land at a distance; and when they came to it, they found it was an island made of water quite surrounded by earth. Besides that, it was bordered by evanescent isthmusses with a great Gulf-stream running about all over it, so that it was perfectly beautiful, and contained only a single tree, 503 feet high.

When they had landed, they walked about, but found to their great surprise, that the island was quite full of veal-cutlets and chocolate-drops, and nothing else. So they all climbed up the single high tree to discover, if possible, if there were any people; but having remained on the top of the tree for a week, and not seeing anybody, they naturally concluded that there were no inhabitants, and accordingly when they came down, they loaded the boat with two thousand veal-cutlets and a million of chocolate drops, and these afforded them sustenance for more than a month, during which time they pursued their voyage with the utmost delight and apathy.

After this they came to a shore where there were no less than sixty-five great red parrots with blue tails, sitting on a rail all of a row, and all fast asleep. And I am sorry to say that the Pussy-cat and the Quangle-Wangle crept softly and bit off the tail-feathers of all the sixty-five parrots, for which Violet reproved them both severely.

Notwithstanding which, she proceeded to insert all the feathers, two hundred and sixty in number, in her bonnet, thereby causing it to have a lovely and glittering appearance, highly prepossessing and efficacious.

The next thing that happened to them was in a narrow part of the sea, which was so entirely full of fishes that the boat could go on no further; so they remained there about six weeks, till they had eaten nearly all the fishes, which were Soles, and all ready-cooked and covered with shrimp sauce, so that there was no trouble whatever. And as the few fishes who remained uneaten complained of the cold, as well as of the difficulty they had in getting any sleep on account of the extreme noise made by the Arctic Bears and the Tropical Turnspits which frequented the neighbourhood in great numbers, Violet most amiably knitted a small woollen frock for several of the fishes, and Slingsby administered some opium drops to them, through which kindness they became quite warm and slept soundly.

Then they came to a country which was wholly covered with immense Orange-trees of a vast size, and quite full of fruit. So they all landed, taking with them the Tea-kettle, intending to gather some of the Oranges and place them in it. But while they were busy about this, a most dreadfully high wind rose, and blew out most of the Parrot-tail feathers from Violet's bonnet. That, however, was nothing compared with the calamity of the

Oranges falling down on their heads by millions and millions, which thumped and bumped and bumped and thumped them all so seriously that they were obliged to run as hard as they could for their lives, besides that the sound of the Oranges rattling on the Tea-kettle was of the most fearful and amazing nature.

Nevertheless they got safely to the boat, although considerably vexed and hurt; and the Quangle-Wangle's right foot was so knocked about, that he had to sit with his head in his slipper for at least a week.

This event made them all for a time rather melancholy, and perhaps they might never have become less so, had not Lionel with a

most praiseworthy devotion and perseverance, continued to stand on one leg and whistle to them in a loud and lively manner, which diverted the whole party so extremely, that they gradually recovered

their spirits, and agreed that whenever they should reach home they would subscribe towards a testimonial to Lionel, entirely made of Gingerbread and Raspberries, as an earnest token of their sincere and grateful infection.

After sailing on calmly for several more days, they came to another country, where they were much pleased and surprised to see a countless multitude of white Mice with red eyes, all sitting in a great circle, slowly eating Custard Pudding with the most satisfactory and polite demeanour.

And as the four Travellers were rather hungry, being tired of

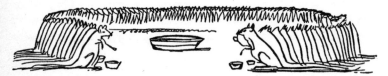

eating nothing but Soles and Oranges for so long a period, they held a council as to the propriety of asking the Mice for some of their Pudding in a humble and affecting manner, by which they could hardly be otherwise than gratified. It was agreed therefore that Guy should go and ask the Mice, which he immediately did; and the result was that they gave a Walnut-shell only half full of Custard diluted with water. Now, this displeased Guy, who said, 'Out of such a lot of Pudding as you have got, I must say you might have spared a somewhat

larger quantity!' But no sooner had he finished speaking than all the Mice turned round at once, and sneezed at him in an appalling and vindictive manner, (and it is impossible to imagine a more scroobious and unpleasant sound than that caused by the simultaneous sneezing of many millions of angry Mice,) so that Guy rushed back to the boat, having first shied his cap into the middle of the Custard Pudding, by which means he completely spoiled the Mice's dinner.

By-and-by the Four Children came to a country where there were no houses, but only an incredibly innumerable number of large bottles without corks, and of a dazzling and sweetly susceptible blue colour. Each of these blue bottles contained a Blue-Bottle Fly, and all these interesting animals live continually together in the most copious and rural harmony, nor perhaps in many parts of the world is such perfect and abject happiness to be found. Violet, and Slingsby, and Guy, and Lionel, were greatly struck with this singular and instructive settlement, and having previously asked permission of the Blue-Bottle-Flies (which was most courteously granted), the Boat was drawn up to the shore and they proceeded to make tea in front of the Bottles; but as they had no tea-leaves, they merely placed some pebbles in the hot

water, and the Quangle-Wangle played some tunes over it on an Accordion, by which of course tea was made directly, and of the very best quality.

The Four Children then entered into conversation with the Blue-Bottle-Flies, who discoursed in a placid and genteel manner, though with a slightly buzzing accent, chiefly owing to the fact that they each held a small clothes-brush between their teeth which naturally occasioned a fizzy extraneous utterance.

'Why,' said Violet, 'would you kindly inform us, do you reside in bottles? and if in bottles at all, why not rather in green or purple, or indeed in yellow bottles?'

To which questions a very aged Blue-Bottle-Fly answered, 'We found the bottles here all ready to live in, that is to say, our great-great-great-great-great-grandfathers did, so we occupied them at once. And when the winter comes on, we turn the bottles upside-down, and consequently rarely feel the cold at all, and you know very well that this could not be the case with bottles of any other colour than blue.'

'Of course it could not;' said Slingsby, 'but if we may take the liberty of inquiring, on what do you chiefly subsist?'

'Mainly on Oyster-patties,' said the Blue-Bottle-Fly, 'and, when these are scarce, on Raspberry Vinegar and Russian leather boiled down to a jelly.'

'How delicious!' said Guy.

To which Lionel added, 'Huzz!' and all the Blue-Bottle-Flies said 'Buzz!'

At this time, an elderly Fly said it was the hour for the Evening-song to be sung; and on a signal being given all the Blue-Bottle-Flies began to buzz at once in a sumptuous and sonorous manner, the melodious and mucilaginous sounds echoing all over the waters, and resounding across the tumultuous tops of the transitory Titmice upon the intervening and verdant mountains, with a serene and sickly suavity only known to the truly virtuous. The Moon was shining slobaciously from the star-bespringled sky, while her light irrigated the smooth and shiny sides and wings and backs of the Blue-Bottle-Flies with a peculiar and trivial splendour, while all nature cheerfully responded to the cerulæan and conspicuous circumstances.

In many long-after years, the four little Travellers looked back to that evening as one of the happiest in all their lives, and it was already past midnight, when—the Sail of the Boat having been set up by the Quangle-Wangle, the Tea-kettle and Ch⸱⸱rn placed in their respective positions, and the Pussy-cat stationed at the Helm—the Children each took a last and affectionate farewell of the Blue-Bottle-Flies, who walked down in a body to the water's edge to see the Travellers embark.

As a token of parting respect and esteem, Violet made a curtsey quite down to the ground, and stuck one of her few remaining Parrot-tail feathers into the back hair of the most pleasing of the Blue-Bottle-

Flies, while Slingsby, Guy, and Lionel offered them three small boxes, containing respectively, Black Pins, Dried Figs, and Epsom Salts: and thus they left that happy shore for ever.

Overcome by their feelings, the Four little Travellers instantly jumped into the Tea-kettle, and fell fast asleep. But all along the shore for many hours there was distinctly heard a sound of severely suppressed sobs, and of a vague multitude of living creatures using their pocket-handkerchiefs in a subdued simultaneous snuffle—lingering sadly along the wallopping waves as the boat sailed farther and farther away from the Land of the Happy Blue-Bottle-Flies.

Nothing particular occurred for some days after these events, except that as the Travellers were passing a low tract of sand, they perceived an unusual and gratifying spectacle, namely, a large number of Crabs and Crawfish—perhaps six or seven hundred—sitting by the water-side, and endeavouring to disentangle a vast heap of pale pink worsted, which they moistened at intervals with a fluid composed of Lavender-water and White-wine Negus.

'Can we be of any service to you, O crusty Crabbies?' said the Four Children.

'Thank you kindly,' said the Crabs, consecutively. 'We are trying to make some worsted Mittens, but do not know how.'

On which Violet, who was perfectly acquainted with the art of mitten-making, said to the Crabs, 'Do your claws unscrew, or are they fixtures?'

'They are all made to unscrew,' said the Crabs, and forthwith they deposited a great pile of claws close to the boat, with which Violet uncombed all the pale pink worsted, and then made the loveliest Mittens with it you can imagine. These the Crabs, having resumed and screwed on their claws, placed cheerfully upon their wrists, and walked away rapidly on their hind-legs, warbling songs with a silvery voice and in a minor key.

After this the four little people sailed on again till they came to a vast and wide plain of astonishing dimensions, on which nothing whatever could be discovered at first; but as the Travellers walked onward, there appeared in the extreme and dim distance a single object, which on a nearer approach and on an accurately cutaneous inspection, seemed to be somebody in a large white wig sitting on an arm-chair made of Sponge Cakes and Oyster-shells. 'It does not quite look like a human being,' said Violet, doubtfully; nor could they make out what it really was, till the Quangle-Wangle (who had previously been round the world), exclaimed softly in a loud voice, 'It is the Co-operative Cauliflower!'

And so in truth it was, and they soon found that what they had taken for an immense wig was in reality the top of the cauliflower, and that he had no feet at all, being able to walk tolerably well with a fluctuating and graceful movement on a single cabbage stalk, an accomplishment which naturally saved him the expense of stockings and shoes.

Presently, while the whole party from the boat was gazing at him with mingled affection and disgust, he suddenly arose, and in a somewhat plumdomphious manner hurried off towards the setting sun,—his steps supported by two superincumbent confidential cucumbers, and a large number of Waterwagtails proceeding in advance of him by three-and-three in a row—till he finally disappeared on the brink of the western sky in a crystal cloud of sudorific sand.

So remarkable a sight of course impressed the Four Children very deeply; and they returned immediately to their boat with a strong sense of undeveloped asthma and a great appetite.

Shortly after this the Travellers were obliged to sail directly below some high overhanging rocks, from the top of one of which, a particularly odious little boy, dressed in rose-coloured knickerbockers, and with a pewter plate upon his head, threw an enormous Pumpkin at the boat, by which it was instantly upset.

But this upsetting was of no consequence, because all the party knew how to swim very well, and in fact they preferred swimming about till after the moon rose, when the water growing chilly, they sponge-taneously entered the boat. Meanwhile the Quangle-Wangle threw back the Pumpkin with immense force, so that it hit the rocks where the malicious little boy in rose-coloured knickerbockers was sitting, when, being quite full of Lucifer-matches, the Pumpkin exploded surreptitiously into a thousand bits, whereon the rocks

instantly took fire, and the odious little boy became unpleasantly hotter and hotter and hotter, till his knickerbockers were turned quite green, and his nose was burned off.

Two or three days after this had happened, they came to another place, where they found nothing at all except some wide and deep pits full of Mulberry Jam. This is the property of the tiny Yellow-nosed Apes who abound in these districts, and who store up the Mulberry Jam for their food in winter, when they mix it with pellucid pale periwinkle soup, and serve it out in Wedgwood China bowls, which grow freely all over that part of the country. Only one of the Yellow-nosed Apes was on the spot, and he was fast asleep: yet the Four Travellers and the Quangle-Wangle and Pussy were so terrified by the violence and sanguinary sound of his snoring, that they merely took a small cupful of the Jam, and returned to re-embark in their Boat without delay.

What was their horror on seeing the boat (including the Churn and the Tea-kettle), in the mouth of an enormous Seeze Pyder, an aquatic and ferocious creature truly dreadful to behold, and happily only met with in those excessive longitudes. In a moment the beautiful boat was bitten into fifty-five-thousand-million-hundred-billion bits, and it instantly became quite clear that Violet, Slingsby, Guy, and Lionel could no longer preliminate their voyage by sea.

The Four Travellers were therefore obliged to resolve on pursuing their wanderings by land, and very fortunately there happened to pass by at that moment, an elderly Rhinoceros, on which they seized; and all four mounting on his back, the Quangle-Wangle sitting on his horn and holding on by his ears, and the Pussy-cat swinging at the end of

his tail, they set off, having only four small beans and three pounds of mashed potatoes to last through their whole journey.

They were, however, able to catch numbers of the chickens and turkeys, and other birds who incessantly alighted on the head of the Rhinoceros for the purpose of gathering the seeds of the rhododendron plants which grew there, and these creatures they cooked in the most translucent and satisfactory manner, by means of a fire lighted on the end of the Rhinoceros' back. A crowd of Kangaroos and Gigantic Cranes accompanied them, from feelings of curiosity and complacency, so that they were never at a loss for company, and went onward as it were in a sort of profuse and triumphant procession.

Thus, in less than eighteen weeks, they all arrived safely at home, where they were received by their admiring relatives with joy tempered with contempt; and where they finally resolved to carry out the rest of their travelling plans at some more favourable opportunity.

As for the Rhinoceros, in token of their grateful adherence, they had him killed and stuffed directly, and then set him up outside the door of their father's house as a Diaphanous Doorscraper.

THE HISTORY OF THE SEVEN FAMILIES
OF THE LAKE PIPPLE-POPPLE

CHAPTER I

INTRODUCTORY

In former days—that is to say, once upon a time, there lived in the Land of Gramblamble, Seven Families. They lived by the side of the great Lake Pipple-popple (one of the Seven Families, indeed, lived *in* the Lake), and on the outskirts of the City of Tosh, which, excepting when it was quite dark, they could see plainly. The names of all these places you have probably heard of, and you have only not to look in your Geography books to find out all about them.

Now the Seven Families who lived on the borders of the great Lake Pipple-popple, were as follows in the next Chapter.

CHAPTER II

THE SEVEN FAMILIES

There was a Family of Two old Parrots and Seven young Parrots.

There was a Family of Two old Storks and Seven young Storks.

There was a Family of Two old Geese, and Seven young Geese.

There was a Family of Two old Owls, and Seven young Owls.

There was a family of Two Old Guinea Pigs and Seven young Guinea Pigs.

There was a Family of Two old Cats and Seven young Cats,

And there was a Family of Two old Fishes and Seven young Fishes.

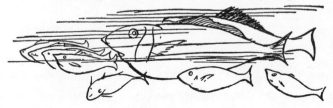

CHAPTER III

THE HABITS OF THE SEVEN FAMILIES

The Parrots lived upon the Soffsky-Poffsky trees,—which were beautiful to behold, and covered with blue leaves,—and they fed upon fruit, artichokes, and striped beetles.

The Storks walked in and out of the Lake Pipple-popple, and ate frogs for breakfast and buttered toast for tea, but on account of the extreme length of their legs, they could not sit down, and so they walked about continually.

The Geese, having webs to their feet, caught quantities of flies, which they ate for dinner.

The Owls anxiously looked after mice, which they caught and made into sago puddings.

The Guinea Pigs toddled about the gardens, and ate lettuces and Cheshire cheese.

The Cats sate still in the sunshine, and fed upon sponge biscuits.

The Fishes lived in the Lake, and fed chiefly on boiled periwinkles.

And all these Seven Families lived together in the utmost fun and felicity.

CHAPTER IV

THE CHILDREN OF THE SEVEN FAMILIES ARE SENT AWAY

One day all the Seven Fathers and the Seven Mothers of the Seven Families agreed that they would send their children out to see the world.

So they called them all together, and gave them each eight shillings and some good advice, some chocolate drops, and a small green morocco pocket-book to set down their expenses in.

They then particularly entreated them not to quarrel, and all the parents sent off their children with a parting injunction.

'If', said the old Parrots, 'you find a Cherry, do not fight about who should have it.'

'And,' said the old Storks, 'if you find a Frog, divide it carefully into seven bits, but on no account quarrel about it.'

And the old Geese said to the Seven young Geese, 'Whatever you do, be sure you do not touch a Plum-pudding Flea.'

And the old Owls said, 'If you find a Mouse, tear him up into seven slices, and eat him cheerfully, but without quarrelling.'

And the old Guinea Pigs said, 'Have a care that you eat your Lettuces, should you find any, not greedily but calmly.'

And the old Cats said, 'Be particularly careful not to meddle with a Clangle-Wangle, if you should see one.'

And the old Fishes said, 'Above all things avoid eating a blue Boss-woss, for they do not agree with Fishes, and give them a pain in their toes.'

So all the Children of each Family thanked their parents, and making in all forty-nine polite bows, they went into the wide world.

CHAPTER V

THE HISTORY OF THE SEVEN YOUNG PARROTS

The Seven young Parrots had not gone far, when they saw a tree with a single Cherry on it, which the oldest Parrot picked instantly, but the other six, being extremely hungry, tried to get it also. On which all the Seven began to fight, and they scuffled,

and huffled,

and ruffled,

and shuffled,

and puffled,

and muffled,

and buffled,

and duffled,

111

and fluffled,
and guffled,
and bruffled, and

screamed, and shrieked, and squealed, and squeaked, and clawed, and snapped, and bit, and bumped, and thumped, and dumped, and flumped each other, till they were all torn into little bits, and at last there was nothing left to record this painful incident, except the Cherry and seven small green feathers.

And that was the vicious and voluble end of the Seven young Parrots.

CHAPTER VI

THE HISTORY OF THE SEVEN YOUNG STORKS

When the Seven young Storks set out, they walked or flew for fourteen weeks in a straight line, and for six weeks more in a crooked one; and after that they ran as hard as they could for one hundred and eight miles: and after that they stood still and made a himmeltanious chatter-clatter-blattery noise with their bills.

About the same time they perceived a large Frog, spotted with green, and with a sky-blue stripe under each ear.

So being hungry, they immediately flew at him, and were going to divide him into seven pieces, when they began to quarrel as to which of his legs should be taken off first. One said this, and another

112

said that, and while they were all quarrelling the Frog hopped away. And when they saw that he was gone, they began to chatter-clatter,

blatter-platter,
patter-blatter,
matter-clatter,
flatter-quatter, more violently

than ever. And after they had fought for a week they pecked each each other all to little pieces, so that at last nothing was left of any of them except their bills,

And that was the end of the Seven young Storks.

CHAPTER VII

THE HISTORY OF THE SEVEN YOUNG GEESE

When the Seven young Geese began to travel, they went over a large plain, on which there was but one tree, and that was a very bad one.

So four of them went up to the top of it, and looked about them, while the other three waddled up and down, and repeated poetry, and their last six lessons in Arithmetic, Geography, and Cookery.

Presently they perceived, a long way off, an object of the most interesting and obese appearance, having a perfectly round body, exactly resembling a boiled plum-pudding, with two little wings, and a beak, and three feathers growing out of his head, and only one leg.

So after a time all the Seven young Geese said to each other, 'Beyond all doubt this beast must be a Plum-pudding Flea!'

On which they incautiously began to sing aloud,

'Plum-pudding Flea,
'Plum-pudding Flea,
'Wherever you be,
'O come to our tree,
'And listen, O listen, O listen to me!'

And no sooner had they sung this verse than the Plum-pudding Flea began to hop and skip on his one leg with the most dreadful velocity, and came straight to the tree, where he stopped and looked about him in a vacant and voluminous manner.

On which the Seven young Geese were greatly alarmed, and all of a tremble-bemble: so one of them put out his long neck, and just touched him with the tip of his bill,—but no sooner had he done this than the Plum-pudding Flea skipped and hopped about more and more and higher and higher, after which he opened his mouth, and, to the great surprise and indignation of the Seven Geese, began to bark so loudly and furiously and terribly that they were totally unable to bear the noise, and by degrees every one of them suddenly tumbled down quite dead.

So that was the end of the Seven young Geese.

CHAPTER VIII

THE HISTORY OF THE SEVEN YOUNG OWLS

When the Seven young Owls set out, they sate every now and then on the branches of old trees, and never went far at one time.

And one night when it was quite dark, they thought they heard a Mouse, but as the gas lamps were not lighted, they could not see him.

So they called out, 'Is that a Mouse?'

On which a Mouse answered, 'Squeaky-peeky-weeky, yes it is.'

And immediately all the young Owls threw themselves off the tree, meaning to alight on the ground; but they did not perceive that there was a large well below them, into which they all fell superficially, and were every one of them drowned in less than half a minute.

So that was the end of the Seven young Owls.

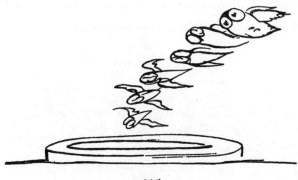

CHAPTER IX

The Seven young Guinea Pigs went into a garden full of Gooseberry-bushes and Tiggory-trees, under one of which they fell asleep. When they awoke, they saw a large Lettuce which had grown out of the ground while they had been sleeping, and which had an immense number of green leaves. At which they all exclaimed,

> 'Lettuce! O Lettuce!
> 'Let us, O let us,
> 'O Lettuce leaves,
> 'O let us leave this tree and eat
> 'Lettuce, O let us, Lettuce leaves!'

And instantly the Seven young Guinea Pigs rushed with such extreme force against the Lettuce-plant, and hit their heads so vividly against its stalk, that the concussion brought on directly an incipient transitional inflammation of their noses, which grew worse and worse and worse and worse till it incidentally killed them all Seven.

And that was the end of the Seven young Guinea Pigs.

116

CHAPTER X

THE HISTORY OF THE SEVEN YOUNG CATS

The Seven young Cats set off on their travels with great delight and rapacity. But, on coming to the top of a high hill, they perceived at a long distance off a Clangle-Wangle (or, as it is more properly written, Clangel-Wangel), and in spite of the warning they had had, they ran straight up to it.

(Now the Clangle-Wangle is a most dangerous and delusive beast, and by no means commonly to be met with. They live in the water as well as on land, using their long tail as a sail when in the former element. Their speed is extreme, but their habits of life are domestic and superfluous, and their general demeanour pensive and pellucid. On summer evenings they may sometimes be observed near the Lake Pipple-popple, standing on their heads and humming their national melodies: they subsist entirely on vegetables, excepting when they eat veal, or mutton, or pork, or beef, or fish, or saltpetre.)

The moment the Clangle-Wangle saw the Seven young Cats approach, he ran away; and as he ran straight on for four months, and the Cats, though they continued to run, could never overtake him,—they all gradually *died* of fatigue and of exhaustion, and never afterwards recovered.

And this was the end of the Seven young Cats.

CHAPTER XI

THE HISTORY OF THE SEVEN YOUNG FISHES

The Seven young fishes swam across the Lake Pipple-popple, and into the river, and into the Ocean, where most unhappily for them, they saw on the 15th day of their travels, a bright blue Boss-Woss, and instantly swam after him. But the Blue Boss-Woss plunged into a perpendicular,

>>spicular,
>>>orbicular,
>>>>quadrangular,
>>>>>circular depth of soft mud,

where in fact his house was.

And the Seven young Fishes, swimming with great and uncomfortable velocity, plunged also into the mud quite against their will, and not being accustomed to it, were all suffocated in a very short period.

And that was the end of the Seven young Fishes.

CHAPTER XII

OF WHAT OCCURRED SUBSEQUENTLY

After it was known that the

>>Seven young Parrots,
>and the Seven young Storks,
>and the Seven young Geese,
>and the Seven young Owls,

118

and the Seven young Guinea Pigs,
and the Seven young Cats,
and the Seven young Fishes,
were all dead, then the Frog, and the Plum-pudding Flea, and the Mouse, and the Clangel Wangel, and the Blue Boss-Woss, all met

together to rejoice over their good fortune. And they collected the Seven Feathers of the Seven young Parrots, and the Seven Bills of the Seven young Storks, and the Lettuce, and the Cherry, and having placed the latter on the Lettuce, and the other objects in a circular arrangement at their base, they danced a hornpipe round all these memorials until they were quite tired: after which they gave a tea-party, and a garden-party, and a ball, and a concert, and then returned to their respective homes full of joy and respect, sympathy, satisfaction, and disgust.

CHAPTER XIII

OF WHAT BECAME OF THE PARENTS OF THE FORTY-NINE CHILDREN

But when the two old Parrots,
and the two old Storks,
and the two old Geese,
and the two old Owls,
and the two old Guinea Pigs,
and the two old Cats,
and the two old Fishes,

became aware by reading in the newspapers, of the calamitous extinction of the whole of their families, they refused all further sustenance; and sending out to various shops, they purchased great quantities of Cayenne Pepper, and Brandy, and Vinegar, and blue Sealing-wax, besides Seven immense glass Bottles with air-tight stoppers. And having done this, they ate a light supper of brown bread and Jerusalem Artichokes, and took an affecting and formal leave of the whole of their acquaintance, which was very numerous and distinguished, and select, and responsible, and ridiculous.

CHAPTER XIV

CONCLUSION

And after this, they filled the bottles with the ingredients for pickling, and each couple jumped into a separate bottle, by which effort of course they all died immediately, and become thoroughly pickled in a few minutes; having previously made their wills (by the assistance of the most eminent Lawyers of the District), in which they left strict orders that the Stoppers of the Seven Bottles should be carefully sealed up with the blue Sealing-wax they had purchased; and that they themselves in the Bottles should be presented to the principal museum of the city of Tosh, to be labelled with Parchment or any other anti-congenial succedaneum, and to be placed on a marble table with silver-gilt legs, for the daily inspection and contemplation, and for the perpetual benefit of the pusillanimous public.

And if ever you happen to go to Gramble-Blamble, and visit that museum in the city of Tosh, look for them on the Ninety-eighth table in the Four hundred and twenty-seventh room of the right-hand corridor of the left wing of the Central Quadrangle of that magnificent building; for if you do not, you certainly will not see them.

NONSENSE COOKERY

Extract from the *Nonsense Gazette*, for August, 1870.

Our readers will be interested in the following communications from our valued and learned contributor, Professor Bosh, whose labours in the fields of Culinary and Botanical science, are so well known to all the world. The first three Articles richly merit to be added to the Domestic cookery of every family; those which follow, claim the attention of all Botanists, and we are happy to be able through Dr. Bosh's kindness to present our readers with illustrations of his discoveries. All the new flowers are found in the valley of Verrikwier, near the lake of Oddgrow, and on the summit of the hill Orfeltugg.'

THREE RECEIPTS FOR DOMESTIC COOKERY

TO MAKE AN AMBLONGUS PIE

Take 4 pounds (say 4½ pounds) of fresh Amblongusses, and put them in a small pipkin.

Cover them with water and boil them for 8 hours incessantly, after which add 2 pints of new milk, and proceed to boil for 4 hours more.

When you have ascertained that the Amblongusses are quite soft, take them out and place them in a wide pan, taking care to shake them well previously.

Grate some nutmeg over the surface, and cover them carefully with powdered gingerbread, curry-powder, and a sufficient quantity of Cayenne papper.

Remove the pan into the next room, and place it on the floor. Bring it back again, and let it simmer for three-quarters of an hour.

Shake the pan violently till all the Amblongusses have become of a pale purple colour.

Then, having prepared the paste, insert the whole carefully, adding at the same time a small pigeon, 2 slices of beef, 4 cauliflowers, and any number of oysters.

Watch patiently till the crust begins to rise, and add a pinch of salt from time to time.

Serve up in a clean dish, and throw the whole out of window as fast as possible.

TO MAKE CRUMBOBBLIOUS CUTLETS

Procure some strips of beef, and having cut them into the smallest possible slices, proceed to cut them still smaller, eight or perhaps nine times.

When the whole is thus minced, brush it up hastily with a new clothes-brush, and stir round rapidly and capriciously with a saltspoon or a soup-ladle.

Place the whole in a saucepan, and remove it to a sunny place,— say the roof of the house if free from sparrows or other birds,—and leave it there for about a week.

At the end of that time add a little lavender, some oil of almonds, and a few herring-bones; and then cover the whole with 4 gallons of clarified crumbobblious sauce, when it will be ready for use.

Cut it into the shape of ordinary cutlets, and serve up in a clean tablecloth or dinner-napkin.

TO MAKE GOSKY PATTIES

Take a Pig, three or four years of age, and tie him by the off-hind leg to a post. Place 5 pounds of currants, 3 of sugar, 2 pecks of peas, 18 roast chestnuts, a candle, and six bushels of turnips, within his reach; if he eats these, constantly provide him with more.

Then procure some cream, some slices of Cheshire cheese, four quires of foolscap paper, and a packet of black pins. Work the whole into a paste, and spread it out to dry on a sheet of clean brown waterproof linen.

When the paste is perfectly dry, but not before, proceed to beat the Pig violently, with the handle of a large broom. If he squeals, beat him again.

Visit the paste and beat the Pig alternately for some days, and ascertain if at the end of that period the whole is about to turn into Gosky Patties.

If it does not then, it never will; and in that case the Pig may be let loose, and the whole process may be considered as finished.

NONSENSE BOTANY

Bottlephorkia Spoonifolia

Smalltoothcombia Domestica

Bluebottlia Buzztilentia

Pollybirdia Singularis

Phattfacia Stupenda

Plumbunnia Nutritiosa

Manypeeplia Upsidownia

Guittara Pensilis

Cockatooca Superba

Baccopipia Gracilis

Fishia Marina

Piggiawiggia Pyramidalis

NONSENSE ALPHABETS

A

A was an ant
Who seldom stood still
And who made a nice house
In the side of a hill.

a !
Nice little Ant!

B

B was a book
With a binding of blue
And pictures and stories
For me and for you.

b !
Nice little Book.

C

C was a cat,
Who ran after a rat
But his courage did fail
When she seized on his tail.

c !
Crafty old Cat!

D

D was a duck
With spots on his back
Who lived in the water
And always said, quack!

d !
Dear little Duck!

E

E was an elephant,
Stately and wise;
He had tusks and a trunk,
And two queer little eyes.

e !
O what funny small eyes!

F

F was a fish,
Who was caught in a net,
But he got out again,
And is quite alive yet.

f !
Lively young Fish!

G

G was a goat
Who was spotted with brown
When he did not lie still,
He walked up and down.

g !
Good little Goat!

H

H was a hat
Which was all on one side,
Its crown was too high
And its brim was too wide.

h !
O! what a Hat!

152

I

I was some ice
So white and so nice
But which nobody tasted,
And so it was wasted.

i !
All that good Ice!

J

J was a jack-daw
Who hopped up and down
In the principal street
Of a neighbouring town.

j !
All through the town!

K

K was a kite
Which flew out of sight
Above houses so high
Quite into the sky.

k !
Fly away, Kite!

L

L was a light
Which burned all the night
And lighted the gloom,
Of a very dark room.

l !
Useful nice light!

M

M was a mill
Which stood on a hill
And turned round and round
With a loud hummy sound.

m !
useful old Mill!

N

N was a net,
Which was thrown in the sea,
To catch fish for dinner
For you and for me.

n !
Nice little Net!

O

O was an orange
So yellow and round;
When it fell off the tree,
It fell down to the ground

o !
Down to the ground!

P

P was a pig
Who was not very big
But his tail was too curly,
And that made him surly.

p !
Cross little Pig!

154

Q

Q was a quail,
With a very short tail
And he fed upon corn
In the evening and morn.

q !
Quaint little Quail.

R

R was a rabbit
Who had a bad habit
Of eating the flowers
In gardens and bowers.

r !
Naughty fat Rabbit!

S

S was the sugar-tongs
Nippity-nee,
To take up the sugar
To put in our tea.

s !
Nippity nee!

T

T was a tortoise
All yellow and black;
He walked slowly away,
And he never came back.

t !
Torty never came back!

U

U was an urn
All polished and bright
And full of hot water
At noon and at night.

u !
Useful old urn!

V

V was a villa
Which stood on a hill
By the side of a river
And close to a mill.

v !
Nice little Villa!

W

W was a whale
With a very long tail
Whose movements were frantic
Across the Atlantic.

w !
Monstrous old Whale!

X

X was King Xerxes,
Who more than all Turks is
Renown'd for his fashion
Of fury and passion.

x !
Angry old Xerxes!

Y

Y was a yew,
Which flourished and grew,
By a quiet abode
Near the side of a road.

y !
Dark little Yew!

Z

Z was some zinc
So shiny and bright,
Which caused you to wink
In the sun's merry light.

z !
Beautiful Zinc!

A

a

A was once an apple-pie,
  Pidy
  Widy
  Tidy
  Pidy
Nice insidy
Apple-Pie.

B

b

B was once a little bear,
  Beary!
  Wary!
  Hairy!
  Beary!
Taky cary!
Little Bear!

C

c

C was once a little cake,
  Caky,
  Baky
  Maky
  Caky,
Taky Caky,
Little Cake!

D

d

D was once a little doll,
  Dolly,
  Molly,
  Polly
  Nolly,
Nursy Dolly,
Little Doll!

E

e

E was once a little eel,
   Eely
   Weely
   Peely
   Eely
Twirly, Tweely
   Little Eel!

F

f

F was once a little fish
   Fishy
   Wishy
   Squishy
   Fishy
In a Dishy
   Little Fish!

G

g

G was once a little goose,
   Goosy
   Moosy
   Boosey
   Goosey
Waddly-woosy
   Little Goose!

H

h

H was once a little hen,
   Henny
   Chenny
   Tenny
   Henny
Eggsy-any
   Little Hen?

I

i

I was once a bottle of ink,
    Inky
    Dinky
    Thinky
    Inky,
Blacky Minky
Bottle of Ink!

J

j

J was once a jar of jam,
    Jammy,
    Mammy,
    Clammy,
    Jammy,
Sweety—Swammy,
    Jar of Jam!

K

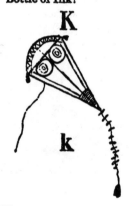

k

K was once a little kite,
    Kity
    Whity
    Flighty
    Kity
Out of Sighty—
Little Kite!

L

l

L was once a little lark,
    Larky!
    Marky!
    Harky!
    Larky!
In the Parky,
Little Lark!

M

m

M was once a little mouse,
    Mousey
    Bousey
    Sousy
    Mousy,
  In the Housy
  Little Mouse!

N

n

N was once a little needle,
    Needly
    Tweedly
    Threedly
    Needly
  Wisky—wheedly
  Little Needle!

O

o

O was once a little owl,
    Owly,
    Prowly,
    Howly,
    Owly
  Browny fowly
  Little Owl!

P

p

P was once a little pump,
    Pumpy
    Slumpy
    Flumpy
    Pumpy
  Dumpy, Thumpy
  Little Pump!

Q

q

Q was once a little quail,
　Quaily
　Faily
　Daily
　Quaily
Stumpy-taily
　Little Quail!

R

r

R was once a little rose,
　Rosy
　Posy
　Nosy
　Rosy
Blows-y—grows-y
　Little Rose!

S

s

S was once a little shrimp
　Shrimpy
　Nimpy
　Flimpy
　Shrimpy
Jumpy—jimpy
　Little Shrimp!

T

t

T was once a little thrush,
　Thrushy!
　Hushy!
　Bushy!
　Thrushy!
Flitty—Flushy—
　Little Thrush!

U

u

U was once a little urn,
   Urny
   Burny
   Turny
   Urny,
Bubbly—burny,
   Little Urn.

V

v

V was once a little vine,
   Viny
   Winy
   Twiny
   Viny
   Twisty-twiny
   Little Vine!

W

w

W was once a whale,
   Whaly
   Scaly
   Shaly
   Whaly
Tumbly-taily
Mighty Whale!

X

x

X was once a great king Xerxes,
   Xerxy
   Perxy
   Turxy
   Xerxy
   Linxy Lurxy
Great King Xerxes!

Y

y

Y was once a little yew,
   Yewdy,
   Fewdy
   Crudy
   Yewdy
Growdy, grewdy,
   Little Yew!

Z

Z

Z was once a piece of zinc
   Tinky
   Winky
   Blinky
   Tinky
Tinkly Minky
Piece of Zinc!

A

A was an ape,
Who stole some white tape
And tied up his toes
In four beautiful bows.

a !
Funny old Ape!

B

B was a bat,
Who slept all the day,
And fluttered about,
When the sun went away.

b !
Brown little bat

C

C was a camel,
You rode on his hump,
And if you fell off,
You come down such a bump!

c !
What a high Camel!

D

D was a dove
Who lived in a wood
With such pretty soft wings,
And so gentle and good.

d !
Dear little Dove!

E

E was an eagle
Who sate on the rocks
And looked down on the fields
And the far away flocks.

e !
Beautiful Eagle!

F

F was a fan
Made of beautiful stuff
And when it was used
It went—Puffy-puff-puff!

f !
Nice little fan.

G

G was a gooseberry
Perfectly red;
To be made into jam
And eaten with bread.

g !
Gooseberry red!

H

H was a heron
Who stood in a stream
The length of his neck
And his legs, was extreme

h !
Long-legged Heron!

I

I was an inkstand
Which stood on a table
With a nice pen to write with,
When we are able!

i !
Neat little inkstand!

J

J was a jug,
So pretty and white
With fresh water in it
At morning and night.

j !
Nice little jug!

K

K was a kingfisher,
Quickly he flew
So bright and so pretty,
Green, purple, and blue.

k !
Kingfisher, blue!

L

L was a lily
So white and so sweet
To see it and smell it
Was quite a nice treat!

l !
Beautiful Lily

147

M

M was a man,
Who walked round and round,
And he wore a long coat
That came down to the ground.

m !
Funny old Man!

N

N was a nut
So smooth and so brown,
And when it was ripe
It fell tumble-dum-down.

n !
Nice little Nut!

O

O was an oyster
Who lived in his shell
If you let him alone
He felt perfectly well.

o !
Open mouth'd Oyster!

P

P was a polly
All red blue and green,
The most beautiful polly
That ever was seen.

p !
Poor little Polly!

Q

Q was a quill
Made into a pen,
But I do not know where
And I cannot say when.

q !
Nice little Quill!

R

R was a rattlesnake
Rolled up so tight
Those who saw him ran quickly
For fear he should bite.

r !
Rattlesnake bite!

S

S was a screw
To screw down a box
And then it was fastened
Without any locks.

s !
Valuable screw!

T

T was a thimble
Of silver so bright
When placed on the finger
It fitted so tight!

t !
Nice little thimble!

U

U was an upper-coat
Woolly and warm
To wear over all
In the snow or the storm.

u !
What a nice upper-coat!

V

V was a veil
With a border upon it
And a riband to tie it
All round a pink bonnet.

v !
Pretty green Veil!

W

W was a watch
Where in letters of gold
The hour of the day
You might always behold.

w !
Beautiful watch!

X

X was King Xerxes
Who wore on his head
A mighty large turban,
Green, yellow, and red.

x !
Look at King Xerxes!

150

Y

Y was a yak
From the land of Thibet,
Except his white tail
He was all black as jet

y !
Look at the Yak!

Z

Z was a zebra,
All striped white and black,
And if he were tame
You might ride on his back.

z !
Pretty striped Zebra!

III

MORE NONSENSE
PICTURES, RHYMES BOTANY
&c.
(1872)

NONSENSE BOTANY

Stunnia Dinnerbellia

Tickia Orologica

Washtubbia Circularis

Tigerlillia Terribilis

Arthbroomia Rigida

Sophtsluggia Glutinosa

Minspysia Deliciosa

Shoebootia Utilis

Jinglia Tinkettlia

Nasticreechia Krorluppia

Enkoopia Chickabiddia

Barkia Howlaloudia

ONE HUNDRED NONSENSE PICTURES AND RHYMES

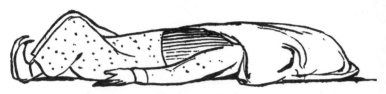

There was an old man of Hong Kong,
Who never did anything wrong;
He lay on his back, with his head in a sack,
That innocuous old man of Hong Kong.

There was an old person of Fife,
Who was greatly disgusted with life;
They sang him a ballad, And fed him on salad,
Which cured that old person of Fife.

159

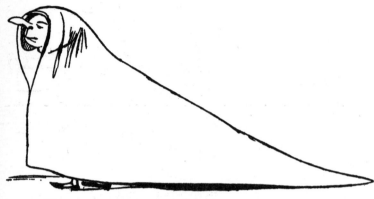

There was a young person in green,
Who seldom was fit to be seen;
She wore a long shawl, over bonnet and all,
Which enveloped that person in green.

There was an old person of Slough,
Who danced at the end of a bough;
But they said, 'If you sneeze, You might damage the trees,
You imprudent old person of Slough.'

There was an old person of Putney,
Whose food was roast spiders and chutney,
Which he took with his tea, within sight of the sea,
That romantic old person of Putney.

There was a young lady in white,
Who looked out at the depths of the night;
But the birds of the air, filled her heart with despair,
And oppressed that young lady in white.

There was an old person of Brill,
Who purchased a shirt with a frill;
But they said, 'Don't you wish, you may'nt look like a fish,
You obsequious old person of Brill?'

There was an old man of Three Bridges,
Whose mind was distracted by midges,
He sate on a wheel, eating underdone veal,
Which relieved that old man of Three Bridges.

There was an old person of Wick,
Who said, 'Tick-a-Tick, Tick-a-Tick;
Chickabee, Chickabaw,' And he said nothing more,
That laconic old person of Wick.

There was a young lady in blue,
Who said, 'Is it you? Is it you?'
When they said, 'Yes, it is,'—She replied only, 'Whizz!'
That ungracious young lady in blue.

163

There was an old person of China,
Whose daughters were Jiska and Dinah,
Amelia and Fluffy, Olivia and Chuffy,
And all of them settled in China.

There was an old man of the Dargle
Who purchased six barrels of Gargle;
For he said, 'I'll sit still, and will roll them down hill,
For the fish in the depths of the Dargle.'

There was an old man in a Marsh,
Whose manners were futile and harsh;
He sate on a log, and sang songs to a frog,
That instructive old man in a Marsh.

There was a young person in red,
Who carefully covered her head,
With a bonnet of leather, and three lines of feather,
Besides some long ribands of red.

There was an old person of Bree,
Who frequented the depths of the sea;
She nurs'd the small fishes, and washed all the dishes,
And swam back again into Bree.

There was an old man in a barge,
Whose nose was exceedingly large;
But in fishing by night, It supported a light,
Which helped that old man in a barge.

166

There was an old person in black,
A Grasshopper jumped on his back;
When it chirped in his ear, He was smitten with fear,
That helpless old person in black.

There was an old man of Toulouse
Who purchased a new pair of shoes;
When they asked, 'Are they pleasant?'—He said, 'Not at present!
That turbid old man of Toulouse.

There was an old man of Blackheath,
Whose head was adorned with a wreath,
Of lobsters and spice, pickled onions and mice,
That uncommon old man of Blackheath.

There was an old man on the Humber,
Who dined on a cake of burnt Uumber;
When he said — 'It's enough!'—They only said, 'Stuff!
You amazing old man on the Humber!'

There was an old person of Stroud,
Who was horribly jammed in a crowd;
Some she slew with a kick, some she scrunched with a stick,
That impulsive old person of Stroud.

There was an old man of Boulak,
Who sate on a Crocodile's back;
But they said, 'Tow'rds the night, he may probably bite,
Which might vex you, old man of Boulak!'

There was an old man of Ibreem,
Who suddenly threaten'd to scream:
But they said, 'If you do, we will thump you quite blue,
You disgusting old man of Ibreem!'

There was an old lady of France,
Who taught little ducklings to dance;
When she said, 'Tick-a-tack!'—They only said, 'Quack!'
Which grieved that old lady of France.

There was an old man who screamed out
Whenever they knocked him about;
So they took off his boots, And fed him with fruits,
And continued to knock him about.

There was an old person of Woking,
Whose mind was perverse and provoking;
He sate on a rail, with his head in a pail,
That illusive old person of Woking.

There was a young person of Bantry,
Who frequently slept in the pantry;
When disturbed by the mice, She appeased them with rice
That judicious young person of Bantry.

There was an Old Man at a Junction,
Whose feelings were wrung with compunction,
When they said 'The Train's gone!' He exclaimed 'How forlorn!'
But remained on the rails of the Junction.

There was an old man, who when little
Fell casually into a kettle;
But, growing too stout, He could never get out,
So he passed all his life in that kettle.

There was an old Lady of Winchelsea,
Who said, 'If you needle or pin shall see,
On the floor of my room, sweep it up with the broom!'
—That exhaustive old Lady of Winchelsea!

There was a young lady of Firle,
Whose hair was addicted to curl;
It curled up a tree, and all over the sea,
That expansive young lady of Firle.

There was an old person of Rye,
Who went up to town on a fly;
But they said, 'If you cough, you are safe to fall off!
You abstemious old person of Rye!'

There was an old man of Messina,
Whose daughter was named Opsibeena;
She wore a small wig, and rode out on a pig,
To the perfect delight of Messina.

There is a young lady, whose nose,
Continually prospers and grows;
When it grew out of sight, she exclaimed in a fright,
'Oh! Farewell to the end of my nose!'

There was an old person of Cannes,
Who purchased three fowls and a fan;
Those she placed on a stool, and to make them feel cool
She constantly fanned them at Cannes.

There was an old person of Barnes,
Whose garments were covered with darns;
But they said, 'Without doubt, you will soon wear them out,
You luminous person of Barnes!'

There was an old man of Cashmere,
Whose movements were scroobious and queer;
Being slender and tall, he looked over a wall,
And perceived two fat ducks of Cashmere.

There was an old person of Hove,
Who frequented the depths of a grove;
Where he studied his books, with the wrens and the rooks,
That tranquil old person of Hove.

There was an old person of Down,
Whose face was adorned with a frown;
When he opened the door, for one minute or more,
He alarmed all the people of Down.

There was an old man of Dunluce,
Who went out to sea on a goose:
When he'd gone out a mile, he observ'd with a smile,
'It is time to return to Dunluce.'

There was a young person of Kew,
Whose virtues and vices were few;
But with blameable haste, she devoured some hot paste,
Which destroyed that young person of Kew.

There was an old person of Sark,
Who made an unpleasant remark;
But they said, 'Don't you see what a brute you must be!'
You obnoxious old person of Sark.

There was an old person of Filey,
Of whom his acquaintance spoke highly;
He danced perfectly well, to the sound of a bell,
And delighted the people of Filey.

There was an old man of El Hums,
Who lived upon nothing but crumbs,
Which he picked off the ground, with the other birds round,
In the roads and the lanes of El Hums.

There was an old man of West Dumpet,
Who possessed a large nose like a trumpet;
When he blew it aloud, it astonished the crowd,
And was heard through the whole of West Dumpet.

There was an old man of Port Grigor,
Whose actions were noted for vigour;
He stood on his head, till his waistcoat turned red,
That eclectic old man of Port Grigor.

There was an old person of Bar,
Who passed all her life in a jar,
Which she painted pea-green, to appear more serene,
That placid old person of Bar.

There was an old person of Pett,
Who was partly consumed by regret;
He sate in a cart, and ate cold apple tart,
Which relieved that old person of Pett.

There was an old person of Newry,
Whose manners were tinctured with fury;
He tore all the rugs, and broke all the jugs
Within twenty miles' distance of Newry.

There was an old person of Jodd,
Whose ways were perplexing and odd;
She purchased a whistle, and sate on a thistle,
And squeaked to the people of Jodd.

There was an old person of Shoreham,
Whose habits were marked by decorum;
He bought an Umbrella, and sate in the cellar,
Which pleased all the people of Shoreham.

There was an old man of Dumbree,
Who taught little owls to drink tea;
For he said, 'To eat mice, is not proper or nice '
That amiable man of Dumbree.

There was an old person of Wilts,
Who constantly walked upon stilts;
He wreathed them with lilies, and daffy-down-dillies,
That elegant person of Wilts.

There was an old man whose remorse,
Induced him to drink Caper Sauce;
For they said, 'If mixed up, with some cold claret-cup,
It will certainly soothe your remorse!'

There was an old person of Cassel,
Whose nose finished off in a tassel;
But they call'd out, 'Oh well!—don't it look like a bell!'
Which perplexed that old person of Cassel.

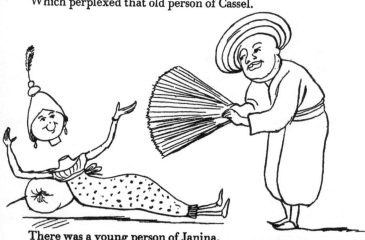

There was a young person of Janina,
Whose uncle was always a fanning her;
When he fanned off her head, she smiled sweetly, and said,
'You propitious old person of Janina!'

There was an old person of Ware,
Who rode on the back of a bear:
When they ask'd,—'Does it trot?'—he said 'Certainly not!
He's a Moppsikon Floppsikon bear!'

There was an old person of Dean
Who dined on one pea, and one bean;
For he said, 'More than that, would make me too fat,'
That cautious old person of Dean.

There was an old person of Dundalk,
Who tried to teach fishes to walk;
When they tumbled down dead, he grew weary, and said,
'I had better go back to Dundalk!'

There was a young person of Ayr,
Whose head was remarkably square:
On the top, in fine weather, she wore a gold feather;
Which dazzled the people of Ayr.

There was an old person of Skye,
Who waltz'd with a Bluebottle fly:
They buzz'd a sweet tune, to the light of the moon,
And entranced all the people of Skye.

There was an old man of Dumblane,
Who greatly resembled a crane;
But they said,—'Is it wrong, since your legs are so long,
To request you won't stay in Dumblane?'

There was an old person of Hyde,
Who walked by the shore with his bride,
Till a Crab who came near, fill'd their bosoms with fear,
And they said, 'Would we'd never left Hyde!'

There was an old person of Rimini,
Who said, 'Gracious! Goodness! O Gimini!'
When they said, 'Please be still!' she ran down a hill,
And was never more heard of at Rimini.

There was an old man in a tree,
Whose whiskers were lovely to see;
But the birds of the air, pluck'd them perfectly bare,
To make themselves nests in that tree.

There was a young lady of Corsica,
Who purchased a little brown saucy-cur;
Which she fed upon ham, and hot raspberry jam,
That expensive young lady of Corsica.

There was an old person of Bray,
Who sang through the whole of the day
To his ducks and his pigs, whom he fed upon figs,
That valuable person of Bray.

There was an old person of Sestri,
Who sate himself down in the vestry,
When they said 'You are wrong!'—he merely said 'Bong!'
That repulsive old person of Sestri.

192

There was an old person of Bude,
Whose deportment was vicious and crude;
He wore a large ruff, of pale straw-coloured stuff,
Which perplexed all the people of Bude.

There was an old person of Bow,
Whom nobody happened to know;
So they gave him some soap, and said coldly, 'We hope
You will go back directly to Bow!'

There was a young lady of Greenwich,
Whose garments were border'd with Spinach;
But a large spotty Calf, bit her shawl quite in half,
Which alarmed that young lady of Greenwich.

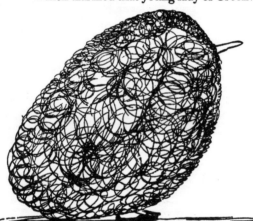

There was an old person of Brigg,
Who purchased no end of a wig;
So that only his nose, and the end of his toes,
Could be seen when he walked about Brigg.

There was an old person of Crowle,
Who lived in the nest of an owl;
When they screamed in the nest, he screamed out with the rest,
That depressing old person of Crowle.

There was an old person in gray,
Whose feelings were tinged with dismay;
She purchased two parrots, and fed them with carrots,
Which pleased that old person in gray.

There was an old person of Blythe,
Who cut up his meat with a scythe;
When they said, 'Well! I never!'--he cried, 'Scythes for ever!'
That lively old person of Blythe.

There was an old person of Ealing,
Who was wholly devoid of good feeling;
He drove a small gig, with three Owls and a Pig,
Which distressed all the people of Ealing.

There was an old person of Ickley,
Who could not abide to ride quickly,
He rode to Karnak, on a tortoise's back,
That moony old person of Ickley.

There was an old man of Ancona,
Who found a small dog with no owner,
Which he took up and down, all the streets of the town;
That anxious old man of Ancona.

There was an old person of Grange,
Whose manners were scroobious and strange;
He sailed to St. Blubb, in a waterproof tub,
That aquatic old person of Grange.

There was an old person of Nice,
Whose associates were usually Geese.
They walked out together, in all sorts of weather.
That affable person of Nice!

198

There was an old person of Deal
Who in walking, used only his heel;
When they said, 'Tell us why?'—He made no reply;
That mysterious old person of Deal.

There was an old man of Thermopylæ,
Who never did anything properly;
But they said, 'If you choose, To boil eggs in your shoes,
You shall never remain in Thermopylæ,'

There was an old person of Minety
Who purchased five hundred and ninety
Large apples and pears, which he threw unawares,
At the heads of the people of Minety.

There was an old man whose despair
Induced him to purchase a hare:
Whereon one fine day, he rode wholly away,
Which partly assuaged his despair.

There was an old person of Pinner,
As thin as a lath, if not thinner;
They dressed him in white, and roll'd him up tight,
That elastic old person of Pinner.

There was an old person of Bromley,
Whose ways were not cheerful or comely;
He sate in the dust, eating spiders and crust,
That unpleasing old person of Bromley.

There was an old man of Dunrose;
A parrot seized hold of his nose.
When he grew melancholy, They said, 'His name's Polly,'
Which soothed that old man of Dunrose.

There was an old man on the Border,
Who lived in the utmost disorder;
He danced with the cat, and made tea in his hat,
Which vexed all the folks on the Border.

There was an old man of Spithead,
Who opened the window, and said,—
'Fil-jomble, fil-jumble, Fil-rumble-come-tumble!'
That doubtful old man of Spithead.

There was an old person of Sheen,
Whose expression was calm and serene;
He sate in the water, and drank bottled porter,
That placid old person of Sheen.

There was an old person of Florence,
Who held mutton chops in abhorrence;
He purchased a Bustard, and fried him in Mustard,
Which choked that old person of Florence.

There was an old person of Loo,
Who said, 'What on earth shall I do?'
When they said, 'Go away!'—she continued to stay,
That vexatious old person of Loo.

There was an old person of Pisa,
Whose daughters did nothing to please her;
She dressed them in gray, and banged them all day,
Round the walls of the city of Pisa.

There was an old man in a garden,
Who always begged every-one's pardon;
When they asked him, 'What for?'—He replied 'You're a bore!
And I trust you'll go out of of my garden.'

205

There was an old man of Thames Ditton,
Who called for something to sit on;
But they brought him a hat, and said—'Sit upon that,
You abruptious old man of Thames Ditton!'

There was an old man of Dee-side
Whose hat was exceedingly wide,
But he said 'Do not fail, If it happen to hail
To come under my hat at Dee-side!'

There was an old man at a Station,
Who made a promiscuous oration;
But they said, 'Take some snuff!—You have talk'd quite enough
You afflicting old man at a Station!'

There was an old person of Shields,
Who frequented the valley and fields;
All the mice and the cats, And the snakes and the rats,
Followed after that person of Shields.

There was a young person in pink,
Who called out for something to drink;
But they said, 'O my daughter, There's nothing but water!'
Which vexed that young person in pink.

There was a young person whose history,
Was always considered a mystery;
She sate in a ditch, although no one knew which,
And composed a small treatise on history.

TWENTY-SIX NONSENSE RHYMES AND PICTURES

The Bountiful Beetle,
who always carried a Green Umbrella when it didn't rain,
and left it at home when it did.

The Comfortable Confidential Cow,
who sate in her Red Morocco Arm Chair and
toasted her own Bread at the parlour Fire.

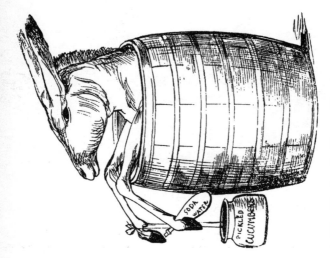

The Absolutely Abstemious Ass,
who resided in a Barrel, and only lived on
Soda Water and Pickled Cucumbers.

The Fizzgiggious Fish,
who always walked about upon Stilts.
because he had no legs.

The Dolomphious Duck,
who caught Spotted Frogs for her dinner
with a Runcible Spoon.

The Enthusiastic Elephant,
who ferried himself across the water with the
Kitchen Poker and a New pair of Ear-rings.

211

The Goodnatured Grey Gull,
who carried the Old Owl, and his Crimson Carpet-bag,
across the river, because he could not swim.

The Hasty Higgeldipiggledy Hen,
who went to market in a Blue Bonnet and Shawl,
and bought a Fish for her Supper.

The Inventive Indian,
who caught a Remarkable Rabbit in a
Stupendous Silver Spoon.

The Judicious Jubilant Jay,
who did up her Back Hair every morning with a Wreath of Roses
Three feathers, and a Gold Pin.

213

The Kicking Kangaroo,
who wore a Pale Pink Muslin dress
with Blue spots.

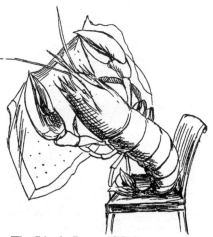

The Lively Learned Lobster,
who mended his own Clothes with
a Needle and Thread.

The Melodious Meritorious Mouse,
who played a merry minuet on the
Piano-forte.

The Nutritious Newt,
who purchased a Round Plum-pudding
for his grand-daughter.

215

The Obsequious Ornamental Ostrich,
who wore Boots to keep his
feet quite dry.

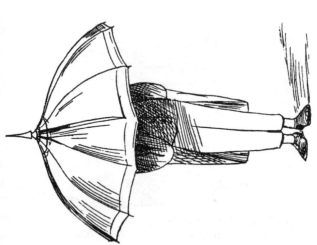

The Umbrageous Umbrella-maker,
whose Face nobody ever saw, because it was
always covered by his Umbrella.

216

The Perpendicular Purple Polly,
who read the Newspaper and ate Parsnip Pie
with his Spectacles.

The Queer Querulous Quail,
who smoked a Pipe of tobacco on the top of
a Tin Tea-kettle.

217

The Rural Runcible Raven,
who wore a White Wig and flew away
with the Carpet Broom.

The Scroobious Snake,
who always wore a Hat on his Head, for
fear he should bite anybody.

218

The Tumultuous Tom-tommy Tortoise,
who beat a Drum all day long in the
middle of the wilderness.

The Visibly Vicious Vulture,
who wrote some Verses to a Veal-cutlet in a
Volume bound in Vellum.

219

The Worrying Whizzing Wasp,
who stood on a Table, and played sweetly on a
Flute with a Morning Cap.

The Excellent Double-extra XX
imbibing King Xerxes, who lived a
long while ago.

The Yonghy-Bonghy-Bo,
whose Head was ever so much bigger than his
Body, and whose Hat was rather small.

The Zigzag Zealous Zebra,
who carried five Monkeys on his back all
the way to Jellibolee.

IV

LAUGHABLE LYRICS
A FOURTH BOOK
OF NONSENSE POEMS, SONGS,
BOTANY MUSIC, &c
(1877)

NONSENSE SONGS

THE DONG WITH A LUMINOUS NOSE

When awful darkness and silence reign
Over the great Gromboolian plain,
   Through the long, long wintry nights;—
When the angry breakers roar
As they beat on the rocky shore;—
   When Storm-clouds brood on the towering heights
Of the Hills of the Chankly Bore:—

Then, through the vast and gloomy dark,
There moves what seems a fiery spark,
   A lonely spark with silvery rays
   Piercing the coal-black night,—
   A Meteor strange and bright:—
Hither and thither the vision strays,
   A single lurid light.

Slowly it wanders,—pauses,—creeps,—
Anon it sparkles,—flashes and leaps;
And ever as onward it gleaming goes
A light on the Bong-tree stems it throws.
And those who watch at that midnight hour
From Hall or Terrace, or lofty Tower,
Cry, as the wild light passes along,—
      'The Dong!—the Dong!
    'The wandering Dong through the forest goes!
      'The Dong! the Dong!
    'The Dong with a luminous Nose!'

      Long years ago
    The Dong was happy and gay,
Till he fell in love with a Jumbly Girl
    Who came to those shores one day,
For the Jumblies came in a sieve, they did,—
Landing at eve near the Zemmery Fidd
    Where the Oblong Oysters grow,
    And the rocks are smooth and gray.
And all the woods and the valleys rang
With the Chorus they daily and nightly sang,—
      'Far and few, far and few,
      Are the lands where the Jumblies live;
      Their heads are green, and their hands are blue
      And they went to sea in a sieve.'

Happily, happily passed those days!
    While the cheerful Jumblies staid;
    They danced in circlets all night long,
    To the plaintive pipe of the lively Dong,
      In moonlight, shine, or shade.
For day and night he was always there

By the side of the Jumbly Girl so fair,
With her sky-blue hands, and her sea-green hair.
Till the morning came of that hateful day
When the Jumblies sailed in their sieve away,
And the Dong was left on the cruel shore
Gazing—gazing for evermore,—
Ever keeping his weary eyes on
That pea-green sail on the far horizon,—
Singing the Jumbly Chorus still
As he sate all day on the grassy hill,—

> *'Far and few, far and few,*
> *Are the lands where the Jumblies live;*
> *Their heads are green, and their hands are blue,*
> *And they went to sea in a sieve.'*

But when the sun was low in the West,
    The Dong arose and said;—
—'What little sense I once possessed
    Has quite gone out of my head!'—
And since that day he wanders still
By lake and forest, marsh and hill,
Singing—'O somewhere, in valley or plain
'Might I find my Jumbly Girl again!
'For ever I'll seek by lake and shore
'Till I find my Jumbly Girl once more!'

> Playing a pipe with silvery squeaks,
> Since then his Jumbly Girl he seeks,
> And because by night he could not see,
> He gathered the bark of the Twangum Tree
>   On the flowery plain that grows.
>   And he wove him a wondrous Nose,—
> A Nose as strange as a Nose could be!

Of vast proportions and painted red,
And tied with cords to the back of his head.
    —In a hollow rounded space it ended
    With a luminous Lamp within suspended,
      All fenced about
      With a bandage stout
      To prevent the wind from blowing it out;—
    And with holes all round to send the light,
    In gleaming rays on the dismal night.

And now each night, and all night long,
Over those plains still roams the Dong;
And above the wail of the Chimp and Snipe
You may hear the squeak of his plaintive pipe
While ever he seeks, but seeks in vain
To meet with his Jumbly Girl again;
Lonely and wild—all night he goes,—
The Dong with a luminous Nose!
And all who watch at the midnight hour,
From Hall or Terrace, or lofty Tower,
Cry, as they trace the Meteor bright,
Moving along through the dreary night,—
    'This is the hour when forth he goes,
    'The Dong with a luminous Nose!
    'Yonder—over the plain he goes;
      'He goes!
      'He goes;
    'The Dong with a luminous Nose!'

THE TWO OLD BACHELORS

Two old Bachelors were living in one house;
One caught a Muffin, the other caught a Mouse.
Said he who caught the Muffin to him who caught the Mouse,—
'This happens just in time! For we've nothing in the house,
'Save a tiny slice of lemon and a teaspoonful of honey,
'And what to do for dinner—since we haven't any money?
'And what can we expect if we haven't any dinner,
'But to lose our teeth and eyelashes and keep on growing thinner?'

Said he who caught the Mouse to him who caught the Muffin,—
'We might cook this little Mouse, if we only had some Stuffin'!
'If we had but Sage and Onion we could do extremely well,
'But how to get that Stuffin' it is difficult to tell'—

Those two old Bachelors ran quickly to the town
And asked for Sage and Onions as they wandered up and down;
They borrowed two large Onions, but no Sage was to be found
In the Shops, or in the Market, or in all the Gardens round.

But some one said,—'A hill there is, a little to the north,
'And to its purpledicular top a narrow way leads forth;—
'And there among the rugged rocks abides an ancient Sage,—
'An earnest Man, who reads all day a most perplexing page.
'Climb up, and seize him by the toes!—all studious as he sits,—
'And pull him down,—and chop him into endless little bits!
'Then mix him with your Onion, (cut up likewise into Scraps,)—
'When your Stuffin' will be ready—and very good: perhaps.'

Those two old Bachelors without loss of time
The nearly purpledicular crags at once began to climb;
And at the top, among the rocks, all seated in a nook,
They saw that Sage, a reading of a most enormous book.

'You earnest Sage!' aloud they cried, 'your book you've read enough
     in!—
'We wish to chop you into bits to mix you into Stuffin'!'—

But that old Sage looked calmly up, and with his awful book,
At those two Bachelors' bald heads a certain aim he took;—
And over Crag and precipice they rolled promiscuous down,—
At once they rolled, and never stopped in lane or field or town,—
And when they reached their house, they found (besides their want
     of Stuffin',)
The Mouse had fled;—and, previously, had eaten up the Muffin.

They left their home in silence by the once convivial door.
And from that hour those Bachelors were never heard of more.

THE PELICANS.

King and Queen of the Peli-cans we, No other birds so grand we see!

None but we have feet like fins with love-ly lea-the-ry throats and chins,

Coro—piu sostenuto.

Ploff-skin, Pluff-skin, Pe-li-can Jee! we think no birds so hap-py as we!

Plump-skin, Ploff-skin, Pe-li-can Jill! We think so then, and we thought so still!

231

THE PELICAN CHORUS

King and Queen of the Pelicans we;
No other Birds so grand we see!
None but we have feet like fins!
With lovely leathery throats and chins!
  Ploffskin, Pluffskin, Pelican jee!
  We think no Birds so happy as we!
  Plumpskin, Ploshkin, Pelican jill!
  We think so then, and we thought so still!

We live on the Nile. The Nile we love.
By night we sleep on the cliffs above;
By day we fish, and at eve we stand
On long bare islands of yellow sand.
And when the sun sinks slowly down
And the great rock walls grow dark and brown,

Where the purple river rolls fast and dim
And the Ivory Ibis starlike skim,
Wing to wing we dance around,—
Stamping our feet with a flumpy sound,—
Opening our mouths as Pelicans ought,
And this is the song we nightly snort;—
    Ploffskin, Pluffskin, Pelican jee,—
    We think no Birds so happy as we!
    Plumpskin, Ploshkin, Pelican jill,—
    We think so then, and we thought so still.

Last year came out our Daughter, Dell;
And all the Birds received her well.
To do her honour, a feast we made
For every bird that can swim or wade.
Herons and Gulls, and Cormorants black,
Cranes, and Flamingoes with scarlet back,
Plovers and Storks, and Geese in clouds,
Swans and Dilberry Ducks in crowds.
Thousands of Birds in wondrous flight!
They ate and drank and danced all night,
And echoing back from the rocks you heard
Multitude-echoes from Bird and Bird,—
    Ploffskin, Pluffskin, Pelican jee,
    We think no Birds so happy as we!
    Plumpskin, Ploshkin, Pelican jill,
    We think so then, and we thought so still!

Yes, they came; and among the rest,
The King of the Cranes all grandly dressed.
Such a lovely tail! Its feathers float
Between the ends of his blue dress-coat;

With pea-green trowsers all so neat,
And a delicate frill to hide his feet,—
(For though no one speaks of it, every one knows,
He has got no webs between his toes!)

As soon as he saw our Daughter Dell,
In violent love that Crane King fell,—
On seeing her waddling form so fair,
With a wreath of shrimps in her short white hair.
And before the end of the next long day,
Our Dell had given her heart away;
For the King of the Cranes had won that heart,
With a Crocodile's egg and a large fish-tart.
She vowed to marry the King of the Cranes,
Leaving the Nile for stranger plains;
And away they flew in a gathering crowd
Of endless birds in a lengthening cloud.
  Ploffskin, Pluffskin, Pelican jee,
   We think no Birds so happy as we!
  Plumpskin, Ploshkin, Pelican jill,
   We think so then, and we thought so still!

And far away in the twilight sky,
We heard them singing a lessening cry,—
Farther and farther till out of sight,
And we stood alone in the silent night!
Often since, in the nights of June,
We sit on the sand and watch the moon;—
She has gone to the great Gromboolian plain,
And we probably never shall meet again!
Oft, in the long still nights of June,
We sit on the rocks and watch the moon;—

————She dwells by the streams of the Chankly Bore,
And we probably never shall see her more.
Ploffskin, Pluffskin, Pelican jee,
We think no Birds so happy as we!
Plumpskin, Ploshkin, Pelican jill,
We think so then, and we thought so still!

Note.—The Air of this and the following Song, by Edward Lear;
the Arrangement for the Piano by Professor Pomè. of Sanremo, Italy.

THE YONGHY BONGHY BÒ.

THE COURTSHIP OF THE YONGHY-
BONGHY-BÒ

I

On the Coast of Coromandel
Where the early pumpkins blow,
In the middle of the woods
  Lived the Yonghy-Bonghy-Bò.
Two old chairs, and half a candle,—
One old jug without a handle,—
    These were all his worldly goods:
    In the middle of the woods,
    These were all the worldly goods,
  Of the Yonghy-Bonghy-Bò,
  Of the Yonghy-Bonghy-Bò.

II

Once, among the Bong-trees walking
  Where the early pumpkins blow,
    To a little heap of stones
  Came the Yonghy-Bonghy-Bò.
There he heard a Lady talking,
To some milk-white Hens of Dorking,—
    ''Tis the Lady Jingly Jones!
    'On that little heap of stones
    'Sits the Lady Jingly Jones!'
  Said the Yonghy-Bonghy-Bò,
  Said the Yonghy-Bonghy-Bò.

III

'Lady Jingly! Lady Jingly!
  'Sitting where the pumpkins blow,
    'Will you come and be my wife?'
  Said the Yonghy-Bonghy-Bò.
'I am tired of living singly,—
'On this coast so wild and shingly,—
    'I'm a-weary of my life:
    'If you'll come and be my wife,
    'Quite serene would be my life!'—
  Said the Yonghy-Bonghy-Bò,
  Said the Yonghy-Bonghy-Bò.

IV

'On this Coast of Coromandel,
  'Shrimps and watercresses grow,
    'Prawns are plentiful and cheap,'
  Said the Yonghy-Bonghy-Bò.
'You shall have my Chairs and candle,

'And my jug without a handle!—
     'Gaze upon the rolling deep
     ('Fish is plentiful and cheap)
     'As the sea, my love is deep!'
Said the Yonghy-Bonghy-Bò,
Said the Yonghy-Bonghy-Bò.

V

Lady Jingly answered sadly,
     And her tears began to flow,—
          'Your proposal comes too late,
     'Mr. Yonghy-Bonghy-Bò!
'I would be your wife most gladly!'
(Here she twirled her fingers madly,)
          'But in England I've a mate!
          'Yes! you've asked me far too late,
          'For in England I've a mate,
     'Mr. Yonghy-Bonghy-Bò!
     'Mr. Yonghy-Bonghy-Bò!'

VI

'Mr. Jones—(his name is Handel,—
     'Handel Jones, Esquire, & Co.)
          'Dorking fowls delights to send,
     'Mr. Yonghy-Bonghy-Bò!
'Keep, oh! keep your chairs and candle,
And your jug without a handle,—
          'I can merely be your friend!
          '—Should my Jones more Dorkings send,
          'I will give you three, my friend!
     'Mr. Yonghy-Bonghy-Bò!
     'Mr. Yonghy-Bonghy-Bò!'

VII

'Though you've such a tiny body,
  'And your head so large doth grow,—
    'Though your hat may blow away,
  'Mr. Yonghy-Bonghy-Bò!
'Though you're such a Hoddy Doddy—
'Yet I wish that I could modi-
    'fy the words I needs must say!
    'Will you please to go away?
    'That is all I have to say—
  'Mr. Yonghy-Bonghy-Bò!
  'Mr. Yonghy-Bonghy-Bò!'

VIII

Down the slippery slopes of Myrtle,
  Where the early pumpkins blow,
    To the calm and silent sea
  Fled the Yonghy-Bonghy-Bò.
There, beyond the Bay of Gurtle,
Lay a large and lively Turtle;—

'You're the Cove,' he said, 'for me
'On your back beyond the sea,
'Turtle, you shall carry me!'
Said the Yonghy-Bonghy-Bò,
Said the Yonghy-Bonghy-Bò.

IX

Through the silent-roaring ocean
Did the Turtle swiftly go;
Holding fast upon his shell
Rode the Yonghy-Bonghy-Bò.
With a sad primæval motion
Towards the sunset isles of Boshen
Still the Turtle bore him well.
Holding fast upon his shell,
'Lady Jingly Jones, farewell!'
Sang the Yonghy-Bonghy-Bò,
Sang the Yonghy-Bonghy-Bò.

X

From the Coast of Coromandel,
Did that Lady never go;
On that heap of stones she mourns
For the Yonghy-Bonghy-Bò.
On that Coast of Coromandel,
In his jug without a handle
Still she weeps, and daily moans;
On that little heap of stones
To her Dorking Hens she moans,
For the Yonghy-Bonghy-Bò,
For the Yonghy-Bonghy-Bò.

THE POBBLE WHO HAS NO TOES

I

The Pobble who has no toes
   Had once as many as we;
When they said, 'Some day you may lose them all;'—
   He replied,—'Fish fiddle de-dee!'
And his Aunt Jobiska made him drink,
Lavender water tinged with pink,
For she said, 'The World in general knows
There's nothing so good for a Pobble's toes!'

II

The Pobble who has no toes,
   Swam across the Bristol Channel;
But before he set out he wrapped his nose,
   In a piece of scarlet flannel.
For his Aunt Jobiska said, 'No harm
'Can come to his toes if his nose is warm;
'And it's perfectly known that a Pobble's toes
'Are safe,—provided he minds his nose.'

The Pobble swam fast and well
   And when boats or ships came near him
He tinkledy-binkledy-winkled a bell
   So that all the world could hear him.
And all the Sailors and Admirals cried,
When they saw him nearing the further side,—
'He has gone to fish, for his Aunt Jobiska's
'Runcible Cat with crimson whiskers!'

IV

But before he touched the shore,
   The shore of the Bristol Channel,
A sea-green Porpoise carried away
   His wrapper of scarlet flannel.
And when he came to observe his feet
Formerly garnished with toes so neat
His face at once became forlorn
On perceiving that all his toes were gone!

V

And nobody ever knew
   From that dark day to the present,
Whoso had taken the Pobble's toes,
   In a manner so far from pleasant.
Whether the shrimps or crawfish gray,
Or crafty Mermaids stole them away—
Nobody knew; and nobody knows
How the Pobble was robbed of his twice five toes!

VI

The Pobble who has no toes
   Was placed in a friendly Bark,

And they rowed him back, and carried him up,
   To his Aunt Jobiska's Park.
And she made him a feast at his earnest wish
Of eggs and buttercups fried with fish;—
And she said,—'It's a fact the whole world knows,
'That Pobbles are happier without their toes.'

THE NEW VESTMENTS

There lived an old man in the Kingdom of Tess,
Who invented a purely original dress;
And when it was perfectly made and complete,
He opened the door, and walked into the street.

By way of a hat, he'd a loaf of Brown Bread,
In the middle of which he inserted his head;—
His Shirt was made up of no end of dead Mice,
The warmth of whose skins was quite fluffy and nice;—
His Drawers were of Rabbit-skins;—so were his Shoes;—
His Stockings were skins,—but it is not known whose;—
His Waistcoat and Trowsers were made of Pork Chops;—
His Buttons were Jujubes, and Chocolate Drops;—
His Coat was all Pancakes with Jam for a border,
And a girdle of Biscuits to keep it in order;
And he wore over all, as a screen from bad weather,
A Cloak of green Cabbage-leaves stitched all together.

He had walked a short way, when he heard a great noise,
Of all sorts of Beasticles, Birdlings, and Boys;—
And from every long street and dark lane in the town
Beasts, Birdles, and Boys in a tumult rushed down.
Two Cows and a half ate his Cabbage-leaf Cloak;—
Four Apes seized his Girdle, which vanished like smoke;—
Three Kids ate up half of his Pancaky Coat,—
And the tails were devour'd by an ancient He Goat;—
An army of Dogs in a twinkling tore *up* his

Pork Waistcoat and Trowsers to give to their Puppies;—
And while they were growling, and mumbling the Chops,
Ten Boys prigged the Jujubes and Chocolate Drops.—
He tried to run back to his house, but in vain,
For Scores of fat Pigs came again and again;—
They rushed out of stables and hovels and doors,—
They tore off his stockings, his shoes, and his drawers;—
And now from the housetops with screechings descend,
Striped, spotted, white, black, and gray Cats without end,
They jumped on his shoulders and knocked off his hat,—
When Crows, Ducks, and Hens made a mincemeat of that;—
They speedily flew at his sleeves in a trice,
And utterly tore up his Shirt of dead Mice;—
They swallowed the last of his Shirt with a squall,—
Whereon he ran home with no clothes on at all.

And he said to himself as he bolted the door,
'I will not wear a similar dress any more,
'Any more, any more, any more, never more!'

MR. AND MRS. DISCOBBOLOS

I

Mr. and Mrs. Discobbolos
   Climbed to the top of a wall.
  And they sate to watch the sunset sky
  And to hear the Nupiter Piffkin cry
   And the Biscuit Buffalo call.
They took up a roll and some Camomile tea,
And both were as happy as happy could be—
      Till Mrs. Discobbolos said,—
      'Oh! W! X! Y! Z!
      'It has just come into my head—
  'Suppose we should happen to fall! ! ! ! !
        'Darling Mr. Discobbolos

II

'Suppose we should fall down flumpetty
   'Just like pieces of stone!
  'On to the thorns,—or into the moat!
  'What would become of your new green coat
   'And might you not break a bone?
'It never occurred to me before—
'That perhaps we shall never go down any more!'
      And Mrs. Discobbolos said—
      'Oh! W! X! Y! Z!
      'What put it into your head
  'To climb up this wall?—my own
        'Darling Mr. Discobbolos?'

III

Mr. Discobbolos answered,—
  'At first it gave me pain,—
 'And I felt my ears turn perfectly pink
 'When your exclamation made me think
  'We might never get down again!
'But now I believe it is wiser far
'To remain for ever just where we are.'—
  And Mr. Discobbolos said,
   'Oh! W! X! Y! Z!
   'It has just come into my head—
'——We shall never go down again—
     'Dearest Mrs. Discobbolos!'

IV

So Mr. and Mrs. Discobbolos
  Stood up, and began to sing,
 'Far away from hurry and strife
'Here we will pass the rest of life,
  'Ding a dong, ding dong, ding!
'We want no knives nor forks nor chairs,
'No tables nor carpets nor household cares,
   'From worry of life we've fled—
   'Oh! W! X! Y! Z!
   'There is no more trouble ahead,
 'Sorrow or any such thing—
     'For Mr. and Mrs. Discobbolos!'

MR. AND MRS. DISCOBBOLOS

SECOND PART

I

Mr. and Mrs. Discobbolos
    Lived on the top of the wall,
  For twenty years, a month and a day,
  Till their hair had grown all pearly gray,
  And their teeth began to fall.
They never were ill, or at all dejected,
By all admired, and by some respected,
    Till Mrs. Discobbolos said,
    'O, W! X! Y! Z!
    'It has just come into my head,
  'We have no more room at all—
                'Darling Mr. Discobbolos!

II

'Look at our six fine boys!
  'And our six sweet girls so fair!
'Upon this wall they have all been born,
'And not one of the twelve has happened to fall
  'Through my maternal care!
'Surely they should not pass their lives
'Without any chance of husbands or wives!'
    And Mrs. Discobbolos said,
    'O, W! X! Y! Z!

'Did it never come into your head
'That our lives must be lived elsewhere,
                    Dearest Mr. Discobbolos?

III

'They have never been at a ball,
  'Nor have even seen a bazaar!
'Nor have heard folks say in a tone all hearty
"What loves of girls (at a garden party)
  Those Misses Discobbolos are!"
'Morning and night it drives me wild
'To think of the fate of each darling child!'
    But Mr. Discobbolos said,
      'O, W! X! Y! Z!
      'What has come to your fiddledum head!
'What a runcible goose you are!
                  'Octopod Mrs. Discobbolos!'

IV

Suddenly Mr. Discobbolos
    Slid from the top of the wall;
  And beneath it he dug a dreadful trench,
  And filled it with dynamite, gunpowder gench,
    And aloud he began to call—
'Let the wild bee sing,
'And the blue bird hum!
'For the end of your lives has certainly come!'
    And Mrs. Discobbolos said,
      'O, W! X! Y! Z!
      'We shall presently all be dead,
  'On this ancient runcible wall,
                  'Terrible Mr. Discobbolos!'
250

Pensively, Mr. Discobbolos
    Sat with his back to the wall;
  He lighted a match, and fired the train,
  And the mortified mountain echoed again
    To the sound of an awful fall!
And all the Discobbolos family flew
In thousands of bits to the sky so blue,
    And no one was left to have said,
    'O, W! X! Y! Z!
    'Has it come into anyone's head
   'That the end has happened to all
             'Of the whole of the Clan Discobbolos?'

THE QUANGLE WANGLE'S HAT

I

On the top of the Crumpetty Tree
  The Quangle Wangle sat,
But his face you could not see,
  On account of his Beaver Hat.
  For his Hat was a hundred and two feet wide,
  With ribbons and bibbons on every side
And bells, and buttons, and loops, and lace,
  So that nobody ever could see the face
        Of the Quangle Wangle Quee.

II

The Quangle Wangle said
  To himself on the Crumpetty Tree,—
'Jam; and jelly; and bread;
  'Are the best food for me!

'But the longer I live on this Crumpetty Tree
'The plainer than ever it seems to me
'That very few people come this way
'And that life on the whole is far from gay!'
        Said the Quangle Wangle Quee.

III

But there came to the Crumpetty Tree,
    Mr. and Mrs. Canary;
And they said,—'Did you ever see
    'Any spot so charmingly airy?
'May we build a nest on your lovely Hat?
Mr. Quangle Wangle, grant us that!
'O please let us come and build a nest
'Of whatever material suits you best,
        'Mr. Quangle Wangle Quee!'

IV

And besides, to the Crumpetty Tree
    Came the Stork, the Duck, and the Owl;
The Snail, and the Bumble-Bee,
    The Frog, and the Fimble Fowl;
(The Fimble Fowl, with a Corkscrew leg;)
And all of them said,—We humbly beg,
'We may build our homes on your lovely Hat,—
'Mr. Quangle Wangle, grant us that!
        'Mr. Quangle Wangle Quee!'

V

And the Golden Grouse came there,
    And the Pobble who has no toes,—
And the small Olympian bear,—
    And the Dong with a luminous nose.

And the Blue Baboon, who played the flute,—
And the Orient Calf from the Land of Tute,—
And the Attery Squash, and the Bisky Bat,—
All came and built on the lovely Hat
        Of the Quangle Wangle Quee.

VI

And the Quangle Wangle said
    To himself on the Crumpetty Tree,—
'When all these creatures move
    'What a wonderful noise there'll be!'
And at night by the light of the Mulberry moon
They danced to the Flute of the Blue Baboon,
On the broad green leaves of the Crumpetty Tree,
And all were as happy as happy could be,
        With the Quangle Wangle Quee.

THE CUMMERBUND

AN INDIAN POEM

I

She sate upon her Dobie,
  To watch the Evening Star,
And all the Punkahs as they passed,
  Cried, 'My! how fair you are!'
Around her bower, with quivering leaves,
  The tall Kamsamahs grew,
And Kitmutgars in wild festoons
  Hung down from Tchokis blue.

II

Below her home the river rolled
  With soft meloobious sound,
Where golden-finned Chuprassies swam,
  In myriads circling round.
Above, on tallest trees remote
  Green Ayahs perched alone,
And all night long the Mussak moan'd
  Its melancholy tone.

III

And where the purple Nullahs threw
  Their branches far and wide,—
And silvery Goreewallahs flew
  In silence, side by side,—

The little Bheesties' twittering cry
   Rose on the flagrant air,
And oft the angry Jampan howled
   Deep in his hateful lair.

IV

She sate upon her Dobie,—
   She heard the Nimmak hum,—
When all at once a cry arose,—
   'The Cummerbund is come!'
In vain she fled:—with open jaws
   The angry monster followed,
And so, (before assistance came,)
   That Lady Fair was swollowed.

V

They sought in vain for even a bone
   Respectfully to bury,—
They said,—'Hers was a dreadful fate!'
   (And Echo answered 'Very.')
They nailed her Dobie to the wall,
   Where last her form was seen,
And underneath they wrote these words,
   In yellow, blue, and green:—

Beware, ye Fair! Ye Fair, beware!
   Nor sit out late at night,—
Lest horrid Cummerbunds should come,
   And swollow you outright.

NOTE.—First published in *Times of India*, Bombay, July, 1874.

THE AKOND OF SWAT

W‌ho, or why, or which, or *what*, Is the Akond of Swat?
Is he tall or short, or dark or fair?
Does he sit on a stool or a sofa or chair,   or SQUAT,
          The Akond of Swat?

Is he wise or foolish, young or old?
Does he drink his soup and his coffee cold,   OR HOT,
          The Akond of Swat?

Does he sing or whistle, jabber or talk,
And when riding abroad does he gallop or walk, or TROT,
          The Akond of Swat?

Does he wear a turban, a fez, or a hat?
Does he sleep on a mattress, a bed, or a mat,   or a COT,
          The Akond of Swat?

When he writes a copy in round-hand size,
Does he cross his T's and finish his I's   with a DOT,
          The Akond of Swat?

Can he write a letter concisely clear
Without a speck or a smudge or smear   or BLOT,
          The Akond of Swat?

Do his people like him extremely well?
Or do they, whenever they can, rebel,   or PLOT,
          At the Akond of Swat?

If he catches them then, either old or young,
Does he have them chopped in pieces or hung,   or *shot*,
          The Akond of Swat?

Do his people prig in the lanes or park?
Or even at times, when days are dark,   GAROTTE?
                                                O the Akond of Swat!

Does he study the wants of his own dominion?
Or doesn't he care for public opinion   a JOT,
                                                The Akond of Swat?

To amuse his mind do his people show him
Pictures, or any one's last new poem,   or WHAT,
                                                For the Akond of Swat?

At night if he suddenly screams and wakes,
Do they bring him only a few small cakes,   or a LOT,
                                                For the Akond of Swat?

Does he live on turnips, tea, or tripe?
Does he like his shawl to be marked with a stripe, or a DOT,
                                                The Akond of Swat?

Does he like to lie on his back in a boat
Like the lady who lived in that isle remote,   SHALLOTT,
                                                The Akond of Swat?

Is he quiet, or always making a fuss?
Is his steward a Swiss or a Swede or a Russ,   or a SCOT,
                                                The Akond of Swat?

Does he like to sit by the calm blue wave?
Or to sleep and snore in a dark green cave,   or a GROTT,
                                                The Akond of Swat?

Does he drink small beer from a silver jug?
Or a bowl? or a glass? or a cup? or a mug?   or a POT.
                                                The Akond of Swat?

Does he beat his wife with a gold-topped pipe,
When she let the gooseberries grow too ripe,   or ROT,
                                                The Akond of Swat?

Does he wear a white tie when he dines with friends,
And tie it neat in a bow with ends,   or a KNOT,
                                                The Akond of Swat?

Does he like new cream, and hate mince-pies?
When he looks at the sun does he wink his eyes,   or NOT,
                                        The Akond of Swat?

Does he teach his subjects to roast and bake?
Does he sail about on an inland lake,   in a YACHT,
                                        The Akond of Swat?

Some one, or nobody, knows I wot
Who or which or why or what

                              Is the Akond of Swat!

For the existence of this potentate see Indian newspapers, *passim.* The proper way to read the verses is to make an immense emphasis on the monosyllabic rhymes, which indeed ought to be shouted out by a chorus.

NONSENSE BOTANY

Armchairia Comfortabilis

Bassia Palealensis

Bubblia Blowpipia

Crabbia Horrida

Knutmigrata Simplice

Tureenia Ladlecum

Puffia Leatherbéllowsa

Queeriflora Babyöides

NONSENSE ALPHABET

A

A was an Area Arch,
  Where washerwomen sat;
They made a lot of lovely starch
  To starch Papa's cravat.

B

B was a Bottle blue,
  Which was not very small;
Papa he filled it full of beer,
  And then he drank it all.

C

C was Papa's gray Cat,
  Who caught a squeaky Mouse;
She pulled him by his twirly tail
  All about the house.

D

D was Papa's white Duck,
  Who had a curly tail;
One day it ate a great fat frog,
  Besides a leetle snail.

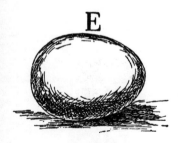

E

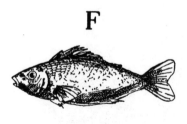

F

E was a little Egg,
   Upon the breakfast table;
Papa came in and ate it up,
   As fast as he was able.

F was a little Fish.
   Cook in the river took it,
Papa said, 'Cook! Cook! bring a dish!
   And, Cook! be quick and cook it!'

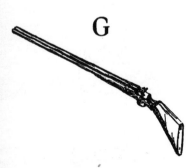

G

H

G was Papa's new Gun;
   He put it in a box;
And then he went and bought a bun,
   And walked about the Docks.

H was Papa's new Hat;
   He wore it on his head;
Outside it was completely black,
   But inside it was red.

I

I was an Inkstand new,
  Papa he likes to use it;
He keeps it in his pocket now,
  For fear that he should lose it.

J

J was some Apple Jam,
  Of which Papa ate part,
But all the rest he took away,
  And stuffed into a tart.

K

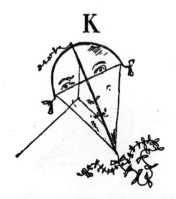

K was a great new Kite;
  Papa he saw it fly
Above a thousand chimney pots,
  And all about the sky.

L

L was a fine new Lamp;
  But when the wick was lit,
Papa he said, 'This light ain't good!
  I cannot read a bit!'

M

M was a dish of Mince;
　　It looked so good to eat!
Papa, he quickly ate it up,
　　And said, 'This is a treat!'

N

N was a Nut that grew
　　High up upon a tree;
Papa, who could not reach it, said,
　　'That's *much* too high for me!'

O

O was an Owl who flew
　　All in the dark away,
Papa said, 'What an owl you are!
　　'Why don't you fly by day!'

P

P was a little Pig,
　　Went out to take a walk;
Papa he said, 'If Piggy dead,
　　He'd all turn into Pork!'

266

Q

Q was a Quince that hung
  Upon a garden tree;
Papa he brought it with him home,
  And ate it with his tea.

R

R was a Railway Rug,
  Extremely large and warm;
Papa he wrapped it round his head,
  In a most dreadful storm.

S

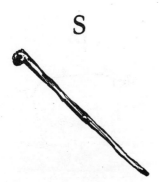

S was Papa's new Stick,
  Papa's new thumping Stick,
To thump extremely wicked boys,
  Because it was so thick.

T

T was a Tumbler full
  Of Punch all hot and good;
Papa he drank it up, when in
  The middle of a wood.

U

U was a silver Urn,
  Full of hot scalding water;
Papa said, 'If that Urn were mine,
  I'd give it to my daughter!'

V

V was a Villain; once
  He stole a piece of beef.
Papa he said, 'O! dreadful man!
  That Villain is a Thief!'

W

W was a Watch of Gold:
  It told the time of day,
So that Papa knew when to come,
  And when to go away.

X

X was King Xerxes, whom
  Papa much wished to know;
But this he could not do, because
  Xerxes died long ago.

Y was a Youth, who kicked
   And screamed and cried like mad;
Papa he said, 'Your conduct is
   Abominably bad!'

Z was a Zebra striped
   And streaked with lines of black;
Papa said once, he thought he'd like
   A ride upon his back.

A   tumbled down, and hurt his Arm, against a bit of wood.

B   said, 'My Boy, O! do not cry; it cannot do you good!'

C   said, 'A Cup of Coffee hot can't do you any harm.'

D   said, 'A Doctor should be fetched, and he would cure the arm.'

E   said, 'An Egg beat up with milk would quickly make him well.'

F   said, 'A Fish, if broiled, might cure, if only by the smell.'

G   said, 'Green Gooseberry fool, the best of cures I hold.'

H   said, 'His Hat should be kept on, to keep him from the cold.'

I   said, 'Some Ice upon his head will make him better soon.'

J   said, 'Some Jam, if spread on bread, or given in a spoon!'

K   said, 'A Kangaroo is here,—this picture let him see.'

L   said, 'A Lamp pray keep alight, to make some barley tea.'

M   said, 'A Mulberry or two might give him satisfaction.'

N   said, 'Some Nuts, if rolled about, might be a slight attraction.'

O   said, 'An Owl might make him laugh, if only it would wink.'

P   said, 'Some Poetry might be read aloud, to make him think.'

Q   said, 'A Quince I recommend,—a Quince, or else a Quail.'

R   said, 'Some Rats might make him move, if fastened by their tail.'

S   said, 'A Song should now be sung, in hopes to make him laugh!'

T   said, 'A Turnip might avail, if sliced or cut in half!'

U   said, 'An Urn, with water hot, place underneath his chin!'

V   said, 'I'll stand upon a chair, and play a Violin!'

W   said, 'Some Whisky-Whizzgigs fetch, some marbles and a ball!'

X   said, 'Some double XX ale would be the best of all!'

Y   said, 'Some Yeast mixed up with salt would make a perfect plaster!'

Z   said, 'Here is a box of Zinc! Get in, my little master!
             'We'll shut you up! We'll nail you down! We will, my little master!
             'We think we've all heard quite enough of this your sad disaster!'

V

NONSENSE SONGS
AND STORIES
(1895)

With the exception of the verses and drawings which follow, this posthumous volume was a selection from the earlier Nonsense Books.

INCIDENTS IN THE LIFE OF MY UNCLE ARLY

I

O My agèd Uncle Arly!
Sitting on a heap of Barley
    Thro' the silent hours of night,—
Close beside a leafy thicket:—
On his nose there was a Cricket,—
In his hat a Railway-Ticket;—
    (But his shoes were far too tight.)

II

Long ago, in youth, he squander'd
All his goods away, and wander'd
    To the Tiniskoop-hills afar.
There on golden sunsets blazing,
Every evening found him gazing,—
Singing,—'Orb! you're quite amazing!
    'How I wonder what you are!'

III

Like the ancient Medes and Persians,
Always by his own exertions
    He subsisted on those hills;—
Whiles,—by teaching children spelling,—
Or at times by merely yelling,—
Or at intervals by selling
    Propter's Nicodemus Pills.'

IV.

Later, in his morning rambles
He perceived the moving brambles—
    Something square and white disclose;—
'Twas a First-class Railway-Ticket;
But, on stooping down to pick it
Off the ground,—a pea-green Cricket
    Settled on my uncle's Nose.

V

Never—never more,—oh! never,
Did that Cricket leave him ever,—
    Dawn or evening, day or night;—
Clinging as a constant treasure,—
Chirping with a cheerious measure,—
Wholly to my uncle's pleasure,—
    (Though his shoes were far too tight.)

VI

So for three-and-forty winters,
Till his shoes were worn to splinters,
    All those hills he wander'd o'er,—
Sometimes silent;—sometimes yelling;—
Till he came to Borley-Melling,
Near his old ancestral dwelling;—
    (But his shoes were far too tight.)

VII

On a little heap of Barley
Died my agèd uncle Arly,
    And they buried him one night;—
Close beside the leafy thicket;—
There,—his hat and Railway-Ticket;—
There,—his ever-faithful Cricket;—
    (But his shoes were far too tight.)

ECLOGUE

COMPOSED AT CANNES, DECEMBER 9TH, 1867

[*Interlocutors*—MR. LEAR AND MR. AND MRS. SYMONDS]

Edwardus.—What makes you look so black, so glum, so cross?
Is it neuralgia, headache, or remorse?

Johannes.—What makes you look as cross, or even more so?
Less like a man than is a broken Torso?

E.—What if my life is odious, should I grin?
If you are savage, need I care a pin?

J.—And if I suffer, am I then an owl?
May I not frown and grind my teeth and growl?

E.—Of course you may; but may not I growl too?
May I not frown and grind my teeth like you?

J.—See Catherine comes! To her, to her,
Let each his several miseries refer;
She shall decide whose woes are least or worst,
And which, as growler, shall rank last or first.

Catherine.—Proceed to growl, in silence I'll attend,
And hear your foolish growlings to the end;
And when they're done, I shall correctly judge

Which of your griefs are real or only fudge.
Begin, let each his mournful voice prepare,
(And, pray, however angry, do not swear!)

J.—We came abroad for warmth, and find sharp cold
    Cannes is an imposition, and we're sold.

E.—Why did I leave my native land, to find
    Sharp hailstones, snow, and most disgusting wind?

J.—What boots it that we orange trees or lemons see,
    If we must suffer from *such* vile inclemency?

E.—Why did I take the lodgings I have got,
    Where all I don't want is:—all I want not?

J.—Last week I called aloud, O! O! O! O!
    The ground is wholly overspread with snow!
    Is that at any rate a theme for mirth
    Which makes a sugar-cake of all the earth?

E.—Why must I sneeze and snuffle, groan and cough,
    If my hat's on my head, or if it's off?
    Why must I sink all poetry in this prose,
    The everlasting blowing of my nose?

J.—When I walk out the mud my footsteps clogs,
    Besides, I suffer from attacks of dogs.

E.—Me a vast awful bulldog, black and brown,
    Completely terrified when near the town;
    As calves, perceiving butchers, trembling reel,
    So did *my* calves the approaching monster feel.

278

J.—Already from two rooms we're driven away,
  Because the beastly chimneys smoke all day:
  Is this a trifle, say? Is this a joke?
  That we, like hams, should be becooked in smoke?

E.—Say! what avails it that my servant speaks
  Italian, English, Arabic, and Greek,
  Besides Albanian: if he don't speak French,
  How can he ask for salt, or shrimps, or tench?

J.—When on the foolish hearth fresh wood I place,
  It whistles, sings, and squeaks, before my face:
  And if it does unless the fire burns bright,
  And if it does, yet squeaks, how can I write?

E.—Alas! I needs must go and call on swells,
  That they may say, 'Pray draw me the Estrelles.'
  On one I went last week to leave a card,
  The swell was out—the servant eyed me hard:
  'This chap's a thief disguised,' his face expressed:
  If I go there again, may I be blest!

J.—Why must I suffer in this wind and gloom?
  Roomattics in a vile cold attic room?

E.—Swells drive about the road with haste and fury,
  As Jehu drove about all over Jewry.
  Just now, while walking slowly, I was all but
  Run over by the Lady Emma Talbot,
  Whom not long since a lovely babe I knew,
  With eyes and cap-ribbons of perfect blue.

J.—Downstairs and upstairs, every blessed minute,
  There's each room with pianofortes in it.

How can I write with noises such as those?
And, being always discomposed, compose?

E.—Seven Germans through my garden lately strayed,
And all on instruments of torture played;
They blew, they screamed, they yelled: how can I paint
Unless my room is quiet, which it ain't?

J.—How can I study if a hundred flies
Each moment blunder into both my eyes?

E.—How can I draw with green or blue or red,
If flies and beetles vex my old bald head?

J.—How can I translate German Metaphys-
Ics, if mosquitoes round my forehead whizz?

E.—I've bought some bacon, (though it's much too fat,)
But round the house there prowls a hideous cat:
Once should I see my bacon in her mouth,
What care I if my rooms look north or south?

J.—Pain from a pane in one cracked window comes,
Which sings and whistles, buzzes, shrieks and hums;
In vain amain with pain the pane with this chord
I fain would strain to stop the beastly *dis*cord!

E.—If rain and wind and snow and such like ills
Continue here, how shall I pay my bills?
For who through cold and slush and rain will come
To see my drawings and to purchase some?
And if they don't, what destiny is mine?
How can I ever get to Palestine?

J.—The blinding sun strikes through the olive trees,
When I walk out, and always makes me sneeze.

E.—Next door, if all night long the moon is shining,
There sits a dog, who wakes me up with whining.

Cath.—Forbear! You both are bores, you've growled enough:
No longer will I listen to such stuff!
All men have nuisances and bores to afflict 'um:
Hark then, and bow to my official dictum!

For you, Johannes, there is most excuse,
(Some interruptions are the very deuce,)
You're younger than the other cove, who surely
Might have some sense—besides, you're somewhat
        poorly.
This therefore is my sentence, that you nurse
The Baby for seven hours, and nothing worse.

For you, Edwardus, I shall say no more
Than that your griefs are fudge, yourself a bore:
Return at once to cold, stewed, minced, hashed mutton—
To wristbands ever guiltless of a button—
To raging winds and sea, (where don't you wish
Your luck may ever let you catch one fish?)—
To make large drawings nobody will buy—
To paint oil pictures which will never dry—
To write new books which nobody will read—
To drink weak tea, on tough old pigs to feed—
Till spring-time brings the birds and leaves and flowers,
And time restores a world of happier hours.

THE HERALDIC BLAZON OF FOSS
THE CAT

[Edward Lear's cat is well known to readers of his letters. Foss was a great pet and lived to the advanced age of seventeen years. He received honourable burial with a suitable inscribed headstone in the garden of Lear's villa at San Remo. *Ed.*]

Fos Couchant

Fos, a untin.

Fes
rampant

Fes dansant

Foss, regardant

Foss Pprpr.

Foss, Passant

285

THE DUCK AND THE KANGAROO
in the autograph of Edward Lear

Said the Duck to the Kangaroo,
  "Good gracious! how you hop!
Over the fields and the water too —
  As if you never would stop!
My life is a bore in this nasty pond
And I long to go out in the world beyond!
  I wish I could hop like you!"
  Said the Duck to the Kangaroo.

"Please give me a ride on your back!"
Said the Duck to the Kangaroo, —
I would sit quite still and say nothing but 'Quack'
  The whole of the long day through!
We would go to the Dee, & the Jelly bo lee
All over the land and over the sea;
  Please take me a ride — o do!"
  Said the Duck to the Kangaroo.

Said the Kangaroo to the Duck, —
 "It requires a little reflection; —
Perhaps on the whole it may bring me luck,
    And there seems but one objection : —
For—(if I'm permitted to speak so bold,)
Your feet are distressingly wet & cold,
       And would certainly give me the rheu=
    = matizz!" said the Kangaroo.

Said the Duck, "As I sat on the rocks
  I thought of all that completely, —
And I bought four pair of worsted socks
    Which fit my, web-feet neatly.
And to keep out the cold I have bought a cloak
And every day a cigar I'll smoke,
        While I follow my own dear true
    = Love of a Kangaroo!"

Said the Kangaroo — "I'm ready — "All in the moonlight pale :—
But to balance me well, o my duck! sit steady,
        And quite at the end of my tail!"
So away they went with a hop and a bound,
And they hopped the whole world 3 times round,
        And who were so happy — oh!! who?
        As the Duck and the Kangaroo.